Docker

For the Absolute Beginner

Christian Leornardo

Table of Contents

Docker Tutorial

This book provides basic and advanced concepts of Docker. Our Docker Tutorial is designed for both beginners as well as professionals.

Docker is a centralized platform for packaging, deploying, and running applications. Before Docker, many users face the problem that a particular code is running in the developer's system but not in the user's system. So, the main reason to develop docker is to help developers to develop applications easily, ship them into containers, and can be deployed anywhere.

Docker was firstly released in March 2013. It is used in the Deployment stage of the software development life cycle that's why it can efficiently resolve issues related to the application deployment.

What is Docker?

Docker is an open source centralized platform designed to create, deploy, and run applications. Docker uses container on the host's operating system to run applications. It allows applications to use the same Linux kernel as a system on the host computer, rather than creating a whole virtual operating system. Containers ensure that our application works in any environment like development, test, or production.

Docker is a container management service. The keywords of Docker are develop, ship and run anywhere. The whole idea of Docker is for developers to easily develop applications, ship them into containers which can then be deployed anywhere.

Components of Docker

Docker has the following components

> ❖ Docker for Mac – It allows one to run Docker containers on the Mac OS.
> ❖ Docker for Linux – It allows one to run Docker containers on the Linux OS.
> ❖ Docker for Windows – It allows one to run Docker containers on the Windows OS.

❖ Docker Engine – It is used for building Docker images and creating Docker containers.
❖ Docker Hub – This is the registry which is used to host various Docker images.
❖ Docker Compose – This is used to define applications using multiple Docker containers.

We will discuss all these components in detail in the subsequent chapters.

The official site for Docker is https://www.docker.com/ The site has all information and documentation about the Docker software. It also has the download links for various operating systems.

Docker includes components such as Docker client, Docker server, Docker machine, Docker hub, Docker composes, etc.

Let's understand the Docker containers and virtual machine.

Docker Containers

Docker containers are the lightweight alternatives of the virtual machine. It allows developers to package up the application with all its libraries and dependencies, and ship it as a single package. The advantage of using a docker container is that you don't need to allocate any RAM and disk space for the applications. It automatically generates storage and space according to the application requirement.

Virtual Machine

A virtual machine is a software that allows us to install and use other operating systems (Windows, Linux, and Debian) simultaneously on our machine. The operating system in which virtual machine runs are called virtualized operating systems. These virtualized operating systems can run programs and preforms tasks that we perform in a real operating system.

Containers Vs. Virtual Machine

Containers	Virtual Machine
Integration in a container is faster and cheap.	Integration in virtual is slow and costly.
No wastage of memory.	Wastage of memory.
It uses the same kernel, but different distribution.	It uses multiple independent operating systems.

Why Docker?

Docker is designed to benefit both the Developer and System Administrator. There are the following reasons to use Docker -

 ❖ Docker allows us to easily install and run software without worrying about setup or dependencies.
 ❖ Developers use Docker to eliminate machine problems, i.e. "but code is worked on my laptop." when working on code together with co-workers.
 ❖ Operators use Docker to run and manage apps in isolated containers for better compute density.
 ❖ Enterprises use Docker to securely built agile software delivery pipelines to ship new application features faster and more securely.
 ❖ Since docker is not only used for the deployment, but it is also a great platform for development, that's why we can efficiently increase our customer's satisfaction.

Advantages of Docker

There are the following advantages of Docker -

 ❖ It runs the container in seconds instead of minutes.
 ❖ It uses less memory.
 ❖ It provides lightweight virtualization.
 ❖ It does not a require full operating system to run applications.
 ❖ It uses application dependencies to reduce the risk.
 ❖ Docker allows you to use a remote repository to share your container with others.
 ❖ It provides continuous deployment and testing environment.

Disadvantages of Docker

There are the following disadvantages of Docker -

- ❖ It increases complexity due to an additional layer.
- ❖ In Docker, it is difficult to manage large amount of containers.
- ❖ Some features such as container self -registration, containers self-inspects, copying files form host to the container, and more are missing in the Docker.
- ❖ Docker is not a good solution for applications that require rich graphical interface.
- ❖ Docker provides cross-platform compatibility means if an application is designed to run in a Docker container on Windows, then it can't run on Linux or vice versa.

Docker Engine

It is a client server application that contains the following major components.

- ❖ A server which is a type of long-running program called a daemon process.
- ❖ The REST API is used to specify interfaces that programs can use to talk to the daemon and instruct it what to do.
- ❖ A command line interface client.

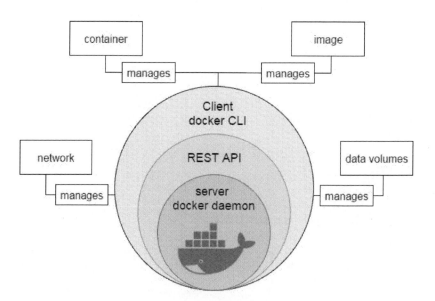

Prerequisite

Before learning Docker, you must have the fundamental knowledge of Linux and programming languages such as java, php, python, ruby, etc.

Audience

Our Docker Tutorial is designed to help beginners and professionals.

Docker Features

❖ Docker has the ability to reduce the size of development by providing a smaller footprint of the operating system via containers.
❖ With containers, it becomes easier for teams across different units, such as development, QA and Operations to work seamlessly across applications.
❖ You can deploy Docker containers anywhere, on any physical and virtual machines and even on the cloud.
❖ Since Docker containers are pretty lightweight, they are very easily scalable.

Although Docker provides lots of features, we are listing some major features which are given below.

❖ Easy and Faster Configuration
❖ Increase productivity
❖ Application Isolation
❖ Swarm
❖ Routing Mesh
❖ Services
❖ Security Management

Easy and Faster Configuration

This is a key feature of docker that helps us to configure the system easily and faster.

We can deploy our code in less time and effort. As Docker can be used in a wide variety of environments, the requirements of the infrastructure are no longer linked with the environment of the application.

Increase productivity

By easing technical configuration and rapid deployment of application. No doubt it has increase productivity. Docker not only helps to execute the application in isolated environment but also it has reduced the resources.

Application Isolation

It provides containers that are used to run applications in isolation environment. Each container is independent to another and allows us to execute any kind of application.

Swarm

It is a clustering and scheduling tool for Docker containers. Swarm uses the Docker API as its front end, which helps us to use various tools to control it. It also helps us to control a cluster of Docker hosts as a single virtual host. It's a self-organizing group of engines that is used to enable pluggable backends.

Routing Mesh

It routes the incoming requests for published ports on available nodes to an active container. This feature enables the connection even if there is no task is running on the node.

Services

Services is a list of tasks that lets us specify the state of the container inside a cluster. Each task represents one instance of a container that should be running and Swarm schedules them across nodes.

Security Management

It allows us to save secrets into the swarm itself and then choose to give services access to certain secrets.

It includes some important commands to the engine like secret inspect, secret create etc.

Docker Architecture

Docker follows client-server architecture. Its architecture consists mainly three parts.

1) Client: Docker provides Command Line Interface (CLI) tools to client to interact with Docker daemon. Client can build, run and stop application. Client can also interact to Docker_Host remotely.

2) Docker_Host: It contains Containers, Images, and Docker daemon. It provides complete environment to execute and run your application.

3) Registry: It is global repository of images. You can access and use these images to run your application in Docker environment.

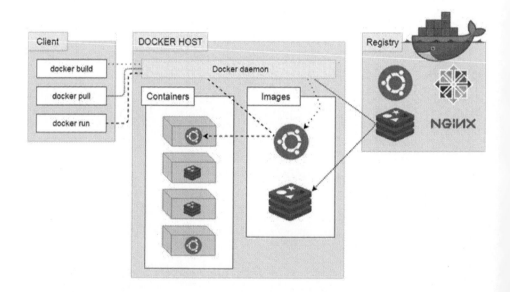

The Docker daemon

It is a process which is used to listen for Docker API requests. It also manages Docker objects like: images, container, network etc. A daemon can also communicate with other daemons to manage Docker services.

The Docker client

The Docker client is the primary way that many Docker users interact with Docker. When we use commands such as docker run, the client sends these commands to docker d, which carries them out. The docker command uses the Docker API.

Docker Registries

Docker registry is used to store Docker images. Docker provides the Docker Hub and the Docker Cloud which are public registries that anyone can use. Docker is configured to look for images on Docker Hub by default.

When we use the docker pull or docker run commands, the required images 4are pulled from your configured registry. When you use the docker push command, your image is pushed to your configured registry.

The following image shows the standard and traditional architecture of virtualization.

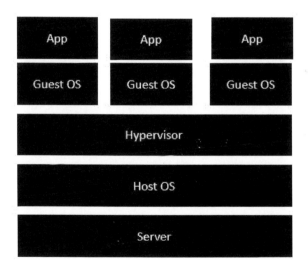

❖ The server is the physical server that is used to host multiple virtual machines.
❖ The Host OS is the base machine such as Linux or Windows.
❖ The Hypervisor is either VMWare or Windows Hyper V that is used to host virtual machines.

❖ You would then install multiple operating systems as virtual machines on top of the existing hypervisor as Guest OS.
❖ You would then host your applications on top of each Guest OS.

The following image shows the new generation of virtualization that is enabled via Dockers. Let's have a look at the various layers.

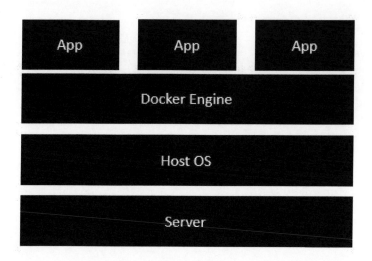

❖ The server is the physical server that is used to host multiple virtual machines. So this layer remains the same.
❖ The Host OS is the base machine such as Linux or Windows. So this layer remains the same.
❖ Now comes the new generation which is the Docker engine. This is used to run the operating system which earlier used to be virtual machines as Docker containers.
❖ All of the Apps now run as Docker containers.

The clear advantage in this architecture is that you don't need to have extra hardware for Guest OS. Everything works as Docker containers.

Docker Installation on Ubuntu

To start the installation of Docker, we are going to use an Ubuntu instance. You can use Oracle Virtual Box to setup a virtual Linux instance, in case you don't have it already.

We can install docker on any operating system whether it is Mac, Windows, Linux or any cloud. Docker Engine runs natively on Linux distributions. Here, we are providing step by step process to install docker engine for Linux Ubuntu Xenial-16.04 [LTS].

Prerequisites:

Docker need two important installation requirements:

- ❖ It only works on a 64-bit Linux installation.
- ❖ It requires Linux kernel version 3.10 or higher.

To check your current kernel version, open a terminal and type *uname -r* command to display your kernel version:

Command:

```
$ uname -r
```

```
● ● ● irfan@irfan-GB-BXBT-2807: ~
irfan@irfan-GB-BXBT-2807:~$ uname -r
4.4.0-59-generic
irfan@irfan-GB-BXBT-2807:~$
```

Update apt sources

Follow following instructions to update apt sources.

1. Open a terminal window.
2. Login as a *root* user by using *sudo* command.
3. Update package information and install CA certificates.

Command:

```
$ apt-get update
$ apt-get install apt-transport-https ca-certificates
```

See, the attached screen shot below.

```
root@ubuntu-pc:/home/pardeep# apt-get install apt-transport-https ca-certificate
s
Reading package lists... Done
Building dependency tree
Reading state information... Done
ca-certificates is already the newest version (20160104ubuntu1).
ca-certificates set to manually installed.
The following packages will be upgraded:
  apt-transport-https
1 upgraded, 0 newly installed, 0 to remove and 345 not upgraded.
Need to get 0 B/26.0 kB of archives.
After this operation, 2,048 B of additional disk space will be used.
Do you want to continue? [Y/n] y
(Reading database ... 181170 files and directories currently installed.)
Preparing to unpack .../apt-transport-https_1.2.18_amd64.deb ...
Unpacking apt-transport-https (1.2.18) over (1.2.10ubuntu1) ...
Setting up apt-transport-https (1.2.18) ...
root@ubuntu-pc:/home/pardeep#
```

4. Add the new GPG key. Following command downloads the key.

Command:

```
$ sudo apt-key adv \
--keyserver hkp://ha.pool.sks-keyservers.net:80 \
--recv-keys 58118E89F3A912897C070ADBF76221572C52609D
```

Screen shot is given below.

```
root@ubuntu-pc:/home/pardeep# sudo apt-key adv \
>              --keyserver hkp://ha.pool.sks-keyservers.net:80 \
>              --recv-keys 58118E89F3A912897C070ADBF76221572C52609D
Executing: /tmp/tmp.1EwmcmFIxB/gpg.1.sh --keyserver
hkp://ha.pool.sks-keyservers.net:80
--recv-keys
58118E89F3A912897C070ADBF76221572C52609D
gpg: requesting key 2C52609D from hkp server ha.pool.sks-keyservers.net
gpg: key 2C52609D: public key "Docker Release Tool (releasedocker) <docker@docke
r.com>" imported
gpg: Total number processed: 1
gpg:              imported: 1  (RSA: 1)
root@ubuntu-pc:/home/pardeep#
```

5. Run the following command, it will substitute the entry for your operating system for the file.

```
$ echo "<REPO>" | sudo tee /etc/apt/sources.list.d/docker.list
```

See, the attached screen shot below.

```
root@ubuntu-pc:/home/pardeep# echo "<REPO>" | sudo tee /etc/apt/sources.list.d/docker.list
<REPO>
```

6. Open the file /etc/apt/sources.list.d/docker.listand paste the following line into the file.

```
deb https://apt.dockerproject.org/repo ubuntu-xenial main
```

```
root@ubuntu-pc:/home/pardeep
deb https://apt.dockerproject.org/repo ubuntu-xenial main
```

7. Now again update your apt packages index.

```
$ sudo atp-get update
```

```
root@ubuntu-pc:/home/pardeep# sudo apt-get update
Hit:1 http://ppa.launchpad.net/clipgrab-team/ppa/ubuntu xenial InRelease
Ign:2 http://dl.google.com/linux/chrome/deb stable InRelease
Hit:3 http://in.archive.ubuntu.com/ubuntu xenial InRelease
Hit:4 http://dl.google.com/linux/chrome/deb stable Release
Hit:5 http://ppa.launchpad.net/nilarimogard/webupd8/ubuntu xenial InRelease
```

See, the attached screen shot below.

8. Verify that APT is pulling from the right repository.

```
$ apt-cache policy docker-engine
```

See, the attached screen shot below.

```
root@ubuntu-pc:/home/pardeep# apt-cache policy docker-engine
docker-engine:
  Installed: (none)
  Candidate: 1.12.6-0~ubuntu-xenial
  Version table:
     1.12.6-0~ubuntu-xenial 500
        500 https://apt.dockerproject.org/repo ubuntu-xenial/main amd64 Packages
     1.12.5-0~ubuntu-xenial 500
        500 https://apt.dockerproject.org/repo ubuntu-xenial/main amd64 Packages
     1.12.4-0~ubuntu-xenial 500
        500 https://apt.dockerproject.org/repo ubuntu-xenial/main amd64 Packages
     1.12.3-0~xenial 500
        500 https://apt.dockerproject.org/repo ubuntu-xenial/main amd64 Packages
     1.12.2-0~xenial 500
```

9. Install the recommended packages.

```
$ sudo apt-get install linux-image-extra-$(uname -
r) linux-image-extra-virtual
```

```
● ● ●   root@ubuntu-pc: /home/pardeep
root@ubuntu-pc:/home/pardeep# sudo apt-get install linux-image-extra-$(uname -r)
linux-image-extra-virtual
Reading package lists... Done
Building dependency tree
Reading state information... Done
linux-image-extra-4.4.0-21-generic is already the newest version (4.4.0-21.37).
linux-image-extra-4.4.0-21-generic set to manually installed.
The following additional packages will be installed:
  linux-generic linux-headers-4.4.0-59 linux-headers-4.4.0-59-generic
  linux-headers-generic linux-image-4.4.0-59-generic
  linux-image-extra-4.4.0-59-generic linux-image-generic
Suggested packages:
  fdutils linux-doc-4.4.0 | linux-source-4.4.0 linux-tools
The following NEW packages will be installed:
  linux-headers-4.4.0-59 linux-headers-4.4.0-59-generic
  linux-image-4.4.0-59-generic linux-image-extra-4.4.0-59-generic
  linux-image-extra-virtual
The following packages will be upgraded:
  linux-generic linux-headers-generic linux-image-generic
3 upgraded, 5 newly installed, 0 to remove and 340 not upgraded.
Need to get 1,768 B/68.4 MB of archives.
After this operation, 296 MB of additional disk space will be used.
Do you want to continue? [Y/n] y
Get:1 http://security.ubuntu.com/ubuntu xenial-security/main amd64 linux-image-e
```

Install the latest Docker version.

1. update your apt packages index.

```
$ sudo apt-get update
```

See, the attached screen shot below.

```
root@ubuntu-pc:/home/pardeep# sudo apt-get update
Hit:1 http://ppa.launchpad.net/clipgrab-team/ppa/ubuntu xenial InRelease
Ign:2 http://dl.google.com/linux/chrome/deb stable InRelease
Hit:3 http://in.archive.ubuntu.com/ubuntu xenial InRelease
Hit:4 http://dl.google.com/linux/chrome/deb stable Release
Hit:5 http://ppa.launchpad.net/nilarimogard/webupd8/ubuntu xenial InRelease
```

2. Install docker-engine.

```
$ sudo apt-get install docker-engine
```

See, the attached screen shot below.

```
root@ubuntu-pc: /home/pardeep
root@ubuntu-pc:/home/pardeep# apt-get install docker-engine
Reading package lists... Done
Building dependency tree
Reading state information... Done
The following additional packages will be installed:
  aufs-tools cgroupfs-mount git git-man liberror-perl
Suggested packages:
  git-daemon-run | git-daemon-sysvinit git-doc git-el git-email git-gui gitk
  gitweb git-arch git-cvs git-mediawiki git-svn
The following NEW packages will be installed:
  aufs-tools cgroupfs-mount docker-engine git git-man liberror-perl
0 upgraded, 6 newly installed, 0 to remove and 340 not upgraded.
Need to get 23.2 MB of archives.
After this operation, 128 MB of additional disk space will be used.
Do you want to continue? [Y/n] y
Get:1 http://in.archive.ubuntu.com/ubuntu xenial/universe amd64 aufs-tools amd64
 1:3.2+20130722-1.1ubuntu1 [92.9 kB]
Get:2 https://apt.dockerproject.org/repo ubuntu-xenial/main amd64 docker-engine
amd64 1.12.6-0~ubuntu-xenial [19.4 MB]
Get:3 http://in.archive.ubuntu.com/ubuntu xenial/universe amd64 cgroupfs-mount a
ll 1.2 [4,970 B]
```

3. Start the docker daemon.

```
$ sudo service docker start
```

See, the attached screen shot below.

```
root@ubuntu-pc:/home/pardeep# service docker start
root@ubuntu-pc:/home/pardeep# █
```

4. Verify that docker is installed correctly by running the hello-world image.

```
$ sudo docker run hello-world
```

See, the attached screen shot below.

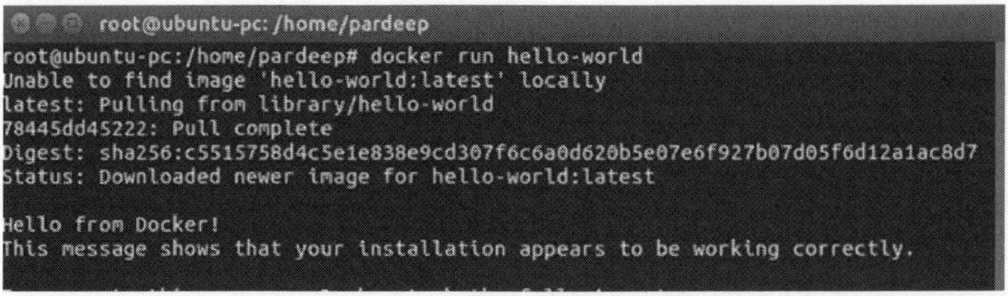

```
● ● ●  root@ubuntu-pc: /home/pardeep
root@ubuntu-pc:/home/pardeep# docker run hello-world
Unable to find image 'hello-world:latest' locally
latest: Pulling from library/hello-world
78445dd45222: Pull complete
Digest: sha256:c5515758d4c5e1e838e9cd307f6c6a0d620b5e07e6f927b07d05f6d12a1ac8d7
Status: Downloaded newer image for hello-world:latest

Hello from Docker!
This message shows that your installation appears to be working correctly.
```

This above command downloads a test image and runs it in a container. When the container runs, it prints a message and exits.

Docker Installation on Windows

We can install docker on any operating system like Windows, Linux, or Mac. Here, we are going to install docker-engine on Windows. The main advantage of using Docker on Windows is that it provides an ability to run natively on Windows without any kind of virtualization. To install docker on windows, we need to download and install the Docker Toolbox.

Follow the below steps to install docker on windows -

Step 1: Click on the below link to download DockerToolbox.exe. https://download.docker.com/win/stable/DockerToolbox.exe

Step 2: Once the DockerToolbox.exe file is downloaded, double click on that file. The following window appears on the screen, in which click on the Next.

Step 3: Browse the location where you want to install the Docker Toolbox and click on the Next.

Step 4: Select the components according to your requirement and click on the Next.

Step 5: Select Additional Tasks and click on the Next.

Step 6: The Docker Toolbox is ready to install. Click on Install.

Step 7: Once the installation is completed, the following Wizard appears on the screen, in which click on the Finish.

Step 8: After the successful installation, three icons will appear on the screen that are: Docker Quickstart Terminal, Kitematic (Alpha), and OracleVM VirtualBox. Double click on the Docker Quickstart Terminal.

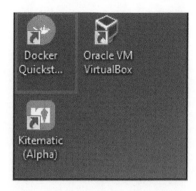

Step 9: A Docker Quickstart Terminal window appears on the screen.

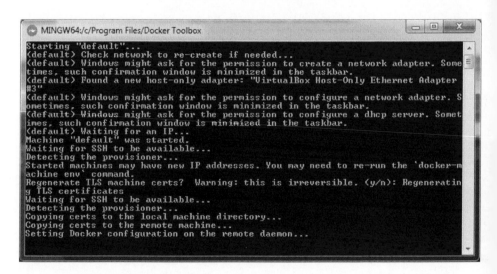

To verify that the docker is successfully installed, type the below command and press enter key.

```
docker run hello-world
```

The following output will be visible on the screen, otherwise not.

```
JTP@JTP-PC MINGW64 /c/Program Files/Docker Toolbox
$ docker run hello-world
Unable to find image 'hello-world:latest' locally
latest: Pulling from library/hello-world
1b930d010525: Pull complete
Digest: sha256:d1668a9a1f5b42ed3f46b70b9cb7c88fd8bdc8a2d73509bb0041cf436018
Status: Downloaded newer image for hello-world:latest

Hello from Docker!
This message shows that your installation appears to be working correctly.

To generate this message, Docker took the following steps:
 1. The Docker client contacted the Docker daemon.
 2. The Docker daemon pulled the "hello-world" image from the Docker Hub.
    (amd64)
 3. The Docker daemon created a new container from that image which runs th
    executable that produces the output you are currently reading.
 4. The Docker daemon streamed that output to the Docker client, which sent
    to your terminal.

To try something more ambitious, you can run an Ubuntu container with:
 $ docker run -it ubuntu bash

Share images, automate workflows, and more with a free Docker ID:
 https://hub.docker.com/

For more examples and ideas, visit:
 https://docs.docker.com/get-started/
```

You can check the Docker version using the following command.

```
docker -version
```

```
JTP@JTP-PC MINGW64 /c/Program Files/Docker Toolbox
$ docker --version
Docker version 18.03.0-ce, build 0520e24302
```

Docker Hub

Docker Hub is a registry service on the cloud that allows you to download Docker images that are built by other communities. You can also upload your own Docker built images to Docker hub. In this chapter, we will see how to download and the use the Jenkins Docker image from Docker hub.

The official site for Docker hub is – https://www.docker.com/community-edition#/add_ons

Step 1 – First you need to do a simple sign-up on Docker hub.

Step 2 – Once you have signed up, you will be logged into Docker Hub.

Step 3 – Next, let's browse and find the Jenkins image.

Step 4 – If you scroll down on the same page, you can see the Docker pull command. This will be used to download the Jenkins image onto the local Ubuntu server.

Step 5 – Now, go to the Ubuntu server and run the following command –

```
sudo docker pull jenkins
```

```
a079defbaeff: Pull complete
66181a89effa: Pull complete
f4d8f7d94b9c: Pull complete
98e5c3e08215: Pull complete
992fde8f3336: Pull complete
65b58e072756: Pull complete
0b0b6d6525a1: Pull complete
4e7171e4505a: Pull complete
469745638476: Pull complete
49d5aaafff78: Pull complete
c01281524fd6: Pull complete
00a759703a0b: Pull complete
da411a858795: Pull complete
7b8a0b4fd7d0: Pull complete
cbd9e145ea6b: Pull complete
700f8f527cd7: Pull complete
88d27231965c: Pull complete
a067af206313: Pull complete
211049e028a4: Pull complete
7249723069d8: Pull complete
6465c437f020: Pull complete
954c67861e66: Pull complete
6a14c8afbb3a: Pull complete
ec070f7e511e: Pull complete
983246da862f: Pull complete
998d1854867e: Pull complete
Digest: sha256:878e055f96c90af9281fd859f7c69ac289e0178594ff36bbb85e53b78969
Status: Downloaded newer image for jenkins:latest
demo@ubuntuserver:~$
demo@ubuntuserver:~$
```

To run Jenkins, you need to run the following command –

```
sudo docker run -p 8080:8080 -p 50000:50000 jenkins
```

Note the following points about the above sudo command –

❖ We are using the sudo command to ensure it runs with root access.

❖ Here, jenkins is the name of the image we want to download from Docker hub and install on our Ubuntu machine.

❖ -p is used to map the port number of the internal Docker image to our main Ubuntu server so that we can access the container accordingly.

```
******************************************************************
******************************************************************

Jenkins initial setup is required. An admin user has been created and a password
 generated.
Please use the following password to proceed to installation:

69a504bd19634390b4e67fdd0a908e67

This may also be found at: /var/jenkins_home/secrets/initialAdminPassword

******************************************************************
******************************************************************
******************************************************************

--> setting agent port for jnlp
--> setting agent port for jnlp... done
Dec 01, 2016 8:16:21 PM hudson.model.UpdateSite updateData
INFO: Obtained the latest update center data file for UpdateSource default
Dec 01, 2016 8:16:22 PM hudson.model.UpdateSite updateData
INFO: Obtained the latest update center data file for UpdateSource default
Dec 01, 2016 8:16:22 PM hudson.model.DownloadService$Downloadable load
INFO: Obtained the updated data file for hudson.tasks.Maven.MavenInstaller
Dec 01, 2016 8:16:22 PM hudson.WebAppMain$3 run
INFO: Jenkins is fully up and running
Dec 01, 2016 8:16:25 PM hudson.model.DownloadService$Downloadable load
INFO: Obtained the updated data file for hudson.tools.JDKInstaller
Dec 01, 2016 8:16:25 PM hudson.model.AsyncPeriodicWork$1 run
INFO: Finished Download metadata. 18,218 ms
```

You will then have Jenkins successfully running as a container on the Ubuntu machine.

Docker Container and Image

Docker container is a running instance of an image. You can use Command Line Interface (CLI) commands to run, start, stop, move, or delete a container. You can also provide configuration for the network and environment variables. Docker container is an isolated and secure application platform, but it can share and access to resources running in a different host or container.

An image is a read-only template with instructions for creating a Docker container. A docker image is described in text file called a Dockerfile, which has a simple, well-defined syntax. An image does not have states and never changes. Docker Engine provides the core Docker technology that enables images and containers.

You can understand container and image with the help of the following command.

```
$ docker run hello-world
```

The above command docker run hello-world has three parts.

1) docker: It is docker engine and used to run docker program. It tells to the operating system that you are running docker program.

2) run: This subcommand is used to create and run a docker container.

3) hello-world: It is a name of an image. You need to specify the name of an image which is to load into the container.

Docker Container

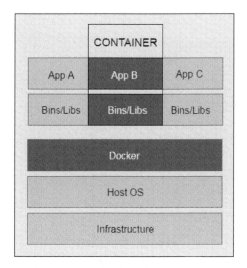

In Docker, everything is based on Images. An image is a combination of a file system and parameters. Let's take an example of the following command in Docker.

```
docker run hello-world
```

- ❖ The Docker command is specific and tells the Docker program on the Operating System that something needs to be done.
- ❖ The run command is used to mention that we want to create an instance of an image, which is then called a container.
- ❖ Finally, "hello-world" represents the image from which the container is made.

Now let's look at how we can use the CentOS image available in Docker Hub to run CentOS on our Ubuntu machine. We can do this by executing the following command on our Ubuntu machine −

```
sudo docker run -it centos /bin/bash
```

Note the following points about the above sudo command −

We are using the sudo command to ensure that it runs with root access.

Here, centos is the name of the image we want to download from Docker Hub and install on our Ubuntu machine.

−it is used to mention that we want to run in interactive mode.

/bin/bash is used to run the bash shell once CentOS is up and running.

Displaying Docker Images

To see the list of Docker images on the system, you can issue the following command.

```
docker images
```

This command is used to display all the images currently installed on the system.

The output below will provide the list of images on the system.

```
sudo docker images
```

When we run the above command, it will produce the following result −

```
demo@ubuntuserver:~$ sudo docker images
[sudo] password for demo:
REPOSITORY         TAG              IMAGE ID          CREATED
VIRTUAL SIZE
newcentos          latest           7a86f8ffcb25      9 days ago
196.5 MB
jenkins            latest           998d1854867e      2 weeks ago
714.1 MB
centos             latest           97cad5e16cb6      4 weeks ago
196.5 MB
demo@ubuntuserver:~$
```

From the above output, you can see that the server has three images: centos, newcentos, and jenkins. Each image has the following attributes −

❖ TAG − This is used to logically tag images.
❖ Image ID − This is used to uniquely identify the image.
❖ Created − The number of days since the image was created.
❖ Virtual Size − The size of the image.

Downloading Docker Images

Images can be downloaded from Docker Hub using the Docker run command. Let's see in detail how we can do this.

The following syntax is used to run a command in a Docker container.

```
docker run image
```

Options

* ❖ Image – This is the name of the image which is used to run the container.

The output will run the command in the desired container.

Example

```
sudo docker run centos
```

This command will download the centos image, if it is not already present, and run the OS as a container.

Output

When we run the above command, we will get the following result –

```
demo@ubuntuserver:~$ sudo docker run centos
Unable to find image 'centos:latest' locally
latest: Pulling from centos

3690474eb5b4: Pull complete
af0819ed1fac: Pull complete
05fe84bf6d3f: Pull complete
97cad5e16cb6: Pull complete
Digest: sha256:934ff980b04db1b7484595bac0c8e6f838e1917ad3a38f904ece64f70bbc
Status: Downloaded newer image for centos:latest
demo@ubuntuserver:~$ _
```

You will now see the CentOS Docker image downloaded. Now, if we run the Docker images command to see the list of images on the system, we should be able to see the centos image as well.

```
demo@ubuntuserver:~$ sudo docker run centos
Unable to find image 'centos:latest' locally
latest: Pulling from centos

3690474eb5b4: Pull complete
af0819ed1fac: Pull complete
05fe84bf6d3f: Pull complete
97cad5e16cb6: Pull complete
Digest: sha256:934ff980b04db1b7484595bac0c8e6f838e1917ad3a38f904ece64f70bbd
Status: Downloaded newer image for centos:latest
demo@ubuntuserver:~$ sudo docker images
REPOSITORY            TAG                 IMAGE ID            CREATED
VIRTUAL SIZE
jenkins               latest              998d1854867e        2 weeks ago
714.1 MB
centos                latest              97cad5e16cb6        4 weeks ago
196.5 MB
demo@ubuntuserver:~$
```

Removing Docker Images

The Docker images on the system can be removed via the docker
rmi command. Let's look at this command in more detail.

▌ docker rmi

This command is used to remove Docker images.

▌ docker rmi ImageID

Options

    ❖ ImageID – This is the ID of the image which needs to be
removed.

Example

▌ sudo docker rmi 7a86f8ffcb25

Here, 7a86f8ffcb25 is the Image ID of the newcentos image.

Output

When we run the above command, it will produce the following result
–

```
demo@ubuntuserver:~$ sudo docker rmi 7a86f8ffcb25
Untagged: newcentos:latest
Deleted: 7a86f8ffcb258e42c11d971a04b1145151b80122e566bc2b544f8fc3f94caf1e
demo@ubuntuserver:~$
```

Let's see some more Docker commands on images.

docker images -q

This command is used to return only the Image ID's of the images.

▌ docker images

Options

q – It tells the Docker command to return the Image ID's only.

The output will show only the Image ID's of the images on the Docker host.

▌ sudo docker images -q

When we run the above command, it will produce the following result –

```
demo@ubuntuserver:~$ sudo docker images -q
998d1854867e
97cad5e16cb6
demo@ubuntuserver:~$ _
```

docker inspect

This command is used see the details of an image or container.

▌ docker inspect Repository

Options

Repository – This is the name of the Image.

The output will show detailed information on the Image.

| sudo docker inspect jenkins

When we run the above command, it will produce the following result –

```
        "Hostname": "6b3797ab1e90",
        "Image": "sha256:532b1ef702484a402708f3b65a61e6ddf307bbf2fdfa01be55
a7678ce6c",
        "Labels": {},
        "MacAddress": "",
        "Memory": 0,
        "MemorySwap": 0,
        "NetworkDisabled": false,
        "OnBuild": [],
        "OpenStdin": false,
        "PortSpecs": null,
        "StdinOnce": false,
        "Tty": false,
        "User": "jenkins",
        "Volumes": {
            "/var/jenkins_home": {}
        },
        "WorkingDir": ""
    },
    "Created": "2016-11-16T20:52:37.5685575092",
    "DockerVersion": "1.12.3",
    "Id": "998d1854867eb7873a9f45ff4c3ab25bcf5378c77fc955d344e47cb27e5df723
    "Os": "linux",
    "Parent": "983246da862f43a967b36cc2fc1af580df3f79760dfd841c1954e7325301
,
    "Size": 5960,
    "VirtualSize": 714121162
}
]
demo@ubuntuserver:~$
```

Docker Containers

Containers are instances of Docker images that can be run using the Docker run command. The basic purpose of Docker is to run containers. Let's discuss how to work with containers.

Running a Container

Running of containers is managed with the Docker run command. To run a container in an interactive mode, first launch the Docker container.

```
sudo docker run -it centos /bin/bash
```

Then hit Crtl+p and you will return to your OS shell.

```
demo@ubuntuserver:~$ sudo docker run -it centos /bin/bash
[root@9f215ed0b0d3 /]#
```

You will then be running in the instance of the CentOS system on the Ubuntu server.

Listing of Containers

One can list all of the containers on the machine via the docker ps command. This command is used to return the currently running containers.

```
docker ps
```

The output will show the currently running containers.

```
sudo docker ps
```

When we run the above command, it will produce the following result –

```
demo@ubuntuserver:~$ sudo docker ps
CONTAINER ID        IMAGE                           COMMAND             CREATED
   STATUS              PORTS                        NAMES
9f215ed0b0d3        centos:latest                   "/bin/bash"         About a minute ago
   Up About a minute                               cocky_colden
demo@ubuntuserver:~$
```

Let's see some more variations of the docker ps command.

▌ docker ps -a

This command is used to list all of the containers on the system

Options

—a — It tells the docker ps command to list all of the containers on the system.

The output will show all containers.

▌ sudo docker ps -a

When we run the above command, it will produce the following result —

```
demo@ubuntuserver:~$ sudo docker ps -a
CONTAINER ID        IMAGE               COMMAND             CREATED
   STATUS                          PORTS
     NAMES
9f215ed0b0d3        centos:latest       "/bin/bash"         4 minutes ago
   Up 4 minutes
     cocky_colden
e5a02936065a        centos:latest       "/bin/bash"         39 minutes ago
   Exited (0) 39 minutes ago
     ecstatic_hodgkin
9b286dd1f16a        jenkins:latest      "/bin/tini -- /usr/l  18 hours ago
   Exited (0) About an hour ago   0.0.0.0:8080->8080/tcp, 0.0.0.0:50000->50000
cp   jolly_wright
3646aa260a2d        jenkins:latest      "/bin/tini -- /usr/l  9 days ago
   Exited (0) 9 days ago          0.0.0.0:8080->8080/tcp, 0.0.0.0:50000->50000
cp   reverent_morse
demo@ubuntuserver:~$ _
```

docker history

With this command, you can see all the commands that were run with an image via a container.

▌ docker history ImageID

Options

ImageID − This is the Image ID for which you want to see all the commands that were run against it.

The output will show all the commands run against that image.

▌ sudo docker history centos

The above command will show all the commands that were run against the centos image.

When we run the above command, it will produce the following result −

```
demo@ubuntuserver:~$ sudo docker images
REPOSITORY              TAG              IMAGE ID         CREATED
VIRTUAL SIZE
jenkins                 latest           998d1854867e     2 weeks ago
714.1 MB
centos                  latest           97cad5e16cb6     4 weeks ago
196.5 MB
demo@ubuntuserver:~$ sudo docker history centos
IMAGE                   CREATED          CREATED BY
        SIZE
97cad5e16cb6            4 weeks ago      /bin/sh -c #(nop)  CMD ["/bin/bash"]
        0 B
05fe84bf6d3f            4 weeks ago      /bin/sh -c #(nop)  LABEL name=CentOS E
e Ima   0 B
af0819ed1fac            4 weeks ago      /bin/sh -c #(nop)  ADD file:54df3580ac9
66389   196.5 MB
3690474eb5b4            3 months ago     /bin/sh -c #(nop)  MAINTAINER https://
thub.   0 B
demo@ubuntuserver:~$ _
```

Building a Web Server Docker File

We have already learnt how to use Docker File to build our own custom images. Now let's see how we can build a web server image which can be used to build containers.

In our example, we are going to use the Apache Web Server on Ubuntu to build our image. Let's follow the steps given below, to build our web server Docker file.

Step 1 − The first step is to build our Docker File. Let's use vim and create a Docker File with the following information.

```
FROM ubuntu
RUN apt-get update
RUN apt-get install -y apache2
RUN apt-get install -y apache2-utils
RUN apt-get clean
EXPOSE 80 CMD ["apache2ctl", "-D", "FOREGROUND"]
```

The following points need to be noted about the above statements −

❖ We are first creating our image to be from the Ubuntu base image.
❖ Next, we are going to use the RUN command to update all the packages on the Ubuntu system.
❖ Next, we use the RUN command to install apache2 on our image.
❖ Next, we use the RUN command to install the necessary utility apache2 packages on our image.
❖ Next, we use the RUN command to clean any unnecessary files from the system.
❖ The EXPOSE command is used to expose port 80 of Apache in the container to the Docker host.
❖ Finally, the CMD command is used to run apache2 in the background.

```
FROM ubuntu
MAINTAINER demousr@gmail.com
RUN apt-get update
RUN apt-get install -y apache2
RUN apt-get install -y apache2-utils
RUN apt-get clean
EXPOSE 80
CMD ["apache2ctl", "-D" , "FOREGROUND"]
```

Now that the file details have been entered, just save the file.

Step 2 – Run the Docker build command to build the Docker file. It
can be done using the following command –

```
sudo docker build -t="mywebserver" .
```

We are tagging our image as mywebserver. Once the image is built,
you will get a successful message that the file has been built.

```
Processing triggers for libc-bin (2.23-0ubuntu5) ...
Processing triggers for systemd (229-4ubuntu12) ...
Processing triggers for sgml-base (1.26+nmu4ubuntu1) ...
 ---> 3deecdb58eea
Removing intermediate container a34fbe45c6f0
Step 5 : RUN apt-get install -y apache2-utils
 ---> Running in 3924b32e72c0
Reading package lists...
Building dependency tree...
Reading state information...
apache2-utils is already the newest version (2.4.18-2ubuntu3.1).
apache2-utils set to manually installed.
0 upgraded, 0 newly installed, 0 to remove and 4 not upgraded.
 ---> 9ddc59d1764b
Removing intermediate container 3924b32e72c0
Step 6 : RUN apt-get clean
 ---> Running in cb73b67c8109
 ---> 4a13c4c36e57
Removing intermediate container cb73b67c8109
Step 7 : EXPOSE 80
 ---> Running in 85245722be33
 ---> e4d2eb0fc674
Removing intermediate container 85245722be33
Step 8 : CMD apache2ctl -D FOREGROUND
 ---> Running in 49d3437f799f
 ---> 5ca8134b8d87
Removing intermediate container 49d3437f799f
Successfully built 5ca8134b8d87
demo@ubuntudemo:~$
```

Step 3 – Now that the web server file has been built, it's now time to
create a container from the image. We can do this with the
Docker run command.

```
sudo docker run -d -p 80:80 mywebserver
```

```
demo@ubuntudemo:~$ sudo docker images
REPOSITORY          TAG               IMAGE ID          CREATED
SIZE
mywebserver         latest            5ca8134b8d87      4 minutes ago
267.6 MB
demousr/demorep     1.0               ab0c1d3744dd      26 hours ago
225.3 MB
ubuntu              latest            104bec311bcd      3 days ago
129 MB
jenkins             latest            ff6f0851ef57      2 weeks ago
714.1 MB
registry            2                 c9bd19d022f6      8 weeks ago
33.3 MB
demo@ubuntudemo:~$ sudo docker run -d -p 80:80 mywebserver
42c70f5e90a2915d1954af2207de75657231c906feb9366f15a4e5c128c0675a
demo@ubuntudemo:~$
```

The following points need to be noted about the above command —

❖   The port number exposed by the container is 80. Hence with the –p command, we are mapping the same port number to the 80 port number on our localhost.
❖   The –d option is used to run the container in detached mode. This is so that the container can run in the background.

If you go to port 80 of the Docker host in your web browser, you will now see that Apache is up and running.

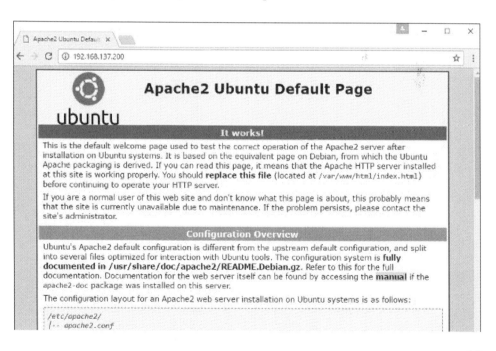

Docker Dockerfile

A Dockerfile is a text document that contains commands that are used Docker Java Application Example to assemble an image. We can use any command that call on the command line. Docker builds images automatically by reading the instructions from the Dockerfile.

The docker build command is used to build an image from the Dockerfile. You can use the -f flag with docker build to point to a Dockerfile anywhere in your file system.

```
$ docker build -f /path/to/a/Dockerfile .
```

Dockerfile Instructions

The instructions are not case-sensitive but you must follow conventions which recommend to use uppercase.

Docker runs instructions of Dockerfile in top to bottom order. The first instruction must be FROM in order to specify the Base Image.

A statement begin with # treated as a comment. You can use RUN, CMD, FROM, EXPOSE, ENV etc instructions in your Dockerfile.

Here, we are listing some commonly used instructions.

FROM

This instruction is used to set the Base Image for the subsequent instructions. A valid Dockerfile must have FROM as its first instruction.

Ex.

```
FROM ubuntu
```

LABEL

We can add labels to an image to organize images of our project. We need to use LABEL instruction to set label for the image.

Ex.

```
LABEL vendorl = "JavaTpoint"
```

RUN

This instruction is used to execute any command of the current image.

Ex.

```
RUN /bin/bash -c 'source $HOME/.bashrc; echo $HOME'
```

CMD

This is used to execute application by the image. We should use CMD always in the following form

```
CMD ["executable", "param1", "param2"?]
```

This is preferred way to use CMD. There can be only one CMD in a Dockerfile. If we use more than one CMD, only last one will execute.

COPY

This instruction is used to copy new files or directories from source to the filesystem of the container at the destination.

Ex.

```
COPY abc/ /xyz
```

Rules

  ❖ The source path must be inside the context of the build. We cannot COPY ../something /something because the first step of a docker build is to send the context directory (and subdirectories) to the docker daemon.
  ❖ If source is a directory, the entire contents of the directory are copied including filesystem metadata.

WORKDIR

The WORKDIR is used to set the working directory for any RUN, CMD and COPY instruction that follows it in the Dockerfile. If work directory does not exist, it will be created by default.

We can use WORKDIR multiple times in a Dockerfile.

Ex.

```
WORKDIR /var/www/html
```

Docker Java Application Example

As, we have mentioned earlier that docker can execute any application.

Here, we are creating a Java application and running by using the docker. This example includes the following steps.

1. Create a directory

Directory is required to organize files. Create a director by using the following command.

```
$ mkdir   java-docker-app
```

See, screen shot for the above command.

```
irfan@irfan-GB-BXBT-2807: ~/Desktop
irfan@irfan-GB-BXBT-2807:~/Desktop$ mkdir java-docker-app
```

2. Create a Java File

Now create a Java file. Save this file as Hello.java file.

// Hello.java

```
class Hello{
public static void main(String[] args){
System.out.println("This is java app \n by using Docker");
}
}
```

Save it inside the directory java-docker-app as Hello.java.

3. Create a Dockerfile

After creating a Java file, we need to create a Dockerfile which contains instructions for the Docker. Dockerfile does not contain any file extension. So, save it simple with Dockerfile name.

// Dockerfile

```
FROM java:8
COPY . /var/www/java
WORKDIR /var/www/java
RUN javac Hello.java
CMD ["java", "Hello"]
```

Write all instructions in uppercase because it is convention. Put this file inside java-docker-app directory. Now we have Dockerfile parallel to Hello.java inside the java-docker-app directory.

See, your folder inside must look like the below.

Dockerfile

Hello.java

4. Build Docker Image

After creating Dockerfile, we are changing working directory.

```
$ cd    java-docker-app
```

See, the screen shot.

```
irfan@irfan-GB-BXBT-2807: ~/Desktop/java-docker-app
irfan@irfan-GB-BXBT-2807:~/Desktop$ cd java-docker-app/
irfan@irfan-GB-BXBT-2807:~/Desktop/java-docker-app$
```

Now, create an image by following the below command. we must login as root in order to create an image. In this example, we have switched to as a root user. In the following command, java-app is name of the image. We can have any name for our docker image.

```
$ docker build -t java-app .
```

See, the screen shot of the above command.

```
root@irfan-GB-BXBT-2807: /home/irfan/Desktop/java-docker-app
root@irfan-GB-BXBT-2807:/home/irfan/Desktop# cd java-docker-app/
root@irfan-GB-BXBT-2807:/home/irfan/Desktop/java-docker-app# docker build -t java-app .
Sending build context to Docker daemon 3.072 kB
Step 1/5 : FROM java:8
 ---> a001fc27db5a
Step 2/5 : COPY . /var/www/html
 ---> Using cache
 ---> 8052cbc8ca31
Step 3/5 : WORKDIR /var/www/html
 ---> Using cache
 ---> 07977e913cb3
Step 4/5 : RUN javac Hello.java
 ---> Using cache
 ---> 0d6e2c3fbd77
Step 5/5 : CMD java Hello
 ---> Using cache
 ---> 3f6fb4241c06
Successfully built 3f6fb4241c06
root@irfan-GB-BXBT-2807:/home/irfan/Desktop/java-docker-app# 
```

After successfully building the image. Now, we can run our docker image.

5. Run Docker Image

After creating image successfully. Now we can run docker by using run command. The following command is used to run java-app.

```
$ docker run java-app
```

See, the screen shot of the above command.

```
root@irfan-GB-BXBT-2807: /home/irfan/Desktop/java-docker-app
root@irfan-GB-BXBT-2807:/home/irfan/Desktop/java-docker-app# docker run java-app
This is java app
 by using Docker
root@irfan-GB-BXBT-2807:/home/irfan/Desktop/java-docker-app# 
```

Here, we can see that after running the java-app it produced an output. Now, we have run docker image successfully on your system. Apart from all these you can also use other commands as well.

Docker Php Application Example

We can run php application using docker. In the following steps, we are creating and running php application.

1. Create a directory

Create a directory to organize files by using following command.

```
$ mkdir php-docker-app
```

See, screen shot of the above command.

```
root@irfan-GB-BXBT-2807: /home/irfan/Desktop/php-docker-app
root@irfan-GB-BXBT-2807:/home/irfan/Desktop# mkdir php-docker-app
root@irfan-GB-BXBT-2807:/home/irfan/Desktop# cd php-docker-app/
root@irfan-GB-BXBT-2807:/home/irfan/Desktop/php-docker-app#
```

2. Create a Php File

// index.php

```
<?php
    echo ?Hello, Php?;
?>
```

3. Create a DockerFile

// Dockefile

```
FROM php:7.0-apache
COPY . /var/www/php
```

After that our project has two files like the below screen-shot.

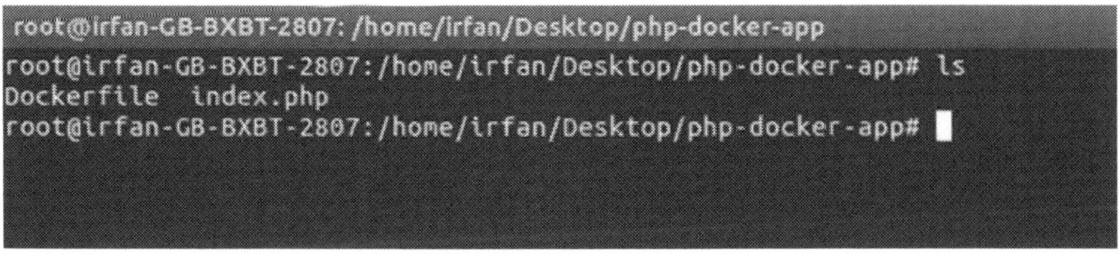

```
root@irfan-GB-BXBT-2807: /home/irfan/Desktop/php-docker-app
root@irfan-GB-BXBT-2807:/home/irfan/Desktop/php-docker-app# ls
Dockerfile  index.php
root@irfan-GB-BXBT-2807:/home/irfan/Desktop/php-docker-app# ▮
```

4. Create Docker Image

$ docker build -t php-app .

In the below screen-shot, we are creating docker image.

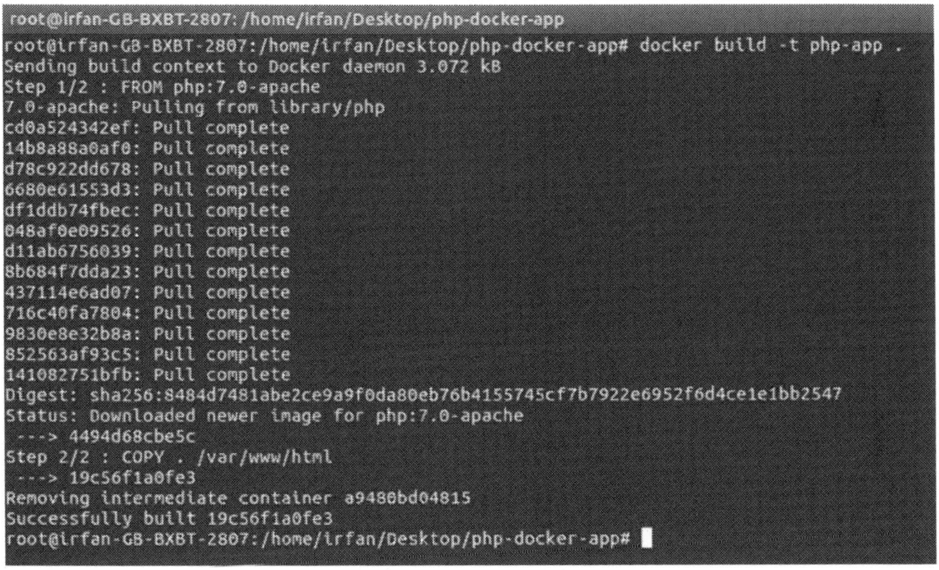

```
root@irfan-GB-BXBT-2807: /home/irfan/Desktop/php-docker-app
root@irfan-GB-BXBT-2807:/home/irfan/Desktop/php-docker-app# docker build -t php-app .
Sending build context to Docker daemon 3.072 kB
Step 1/2 : FROM php:7.0-apache
7.0-apache: Pulling from library/php
cd0a524342ef: Pull complete
14b8a88a0af0: Pull complete
d78c922dd678: Pull complete
6680e61553d3: Pull complete
df1ddb74fbec: Pull complete
048af0e09526: Pull complete
d11ab6756039: Pull complete
8b684f7dda23: Pull complete
437114e6ad07: Pull complete
716c40fa7804: Pull complete
9830e8e32b8a: Pull complete
852563af93c5: Pull complete
141082751bfb: Pull complete
Digest: sha256:8484d7481abe2ce9a9f0da80eb76b4155745cf7b7922e6952f6d4ce1e1bb2547
Status: Downloaded newer image for php:7.0-apache
 ---> 4494d68cbe5c
Step 2/2 : COPY . /var/www/html
 ---> 19c56f1a0fe3
Removing intermediate container a9480bd04815
Successfully built 19c56f1a0fe3
root@irfan-GB-BXBT-2807:/home/irfan/Desktop/php-docker-app# ▮
```

Now look for the available images in the docker container.

```
root@irfan-GB-BXBT-2807:/home/irfan/Desktop/php-docker-app# docker images
REPOSITORY          TAG             IMAGE ID        CREATED             SIZE
php-app             latest          19c56f1a0fe3    13 minutes ago      385 MB
php                 7.0-apache      4494d68cbe5c    About an hour ago   385 MB
root@irfan-GB-BXBT-2807:/home/irfan/Desktop/php-docker-app# ▮
```

The above screen-shot shows that the created image php-app is available.

5. Run the Docker image

Now run the docker image. The following command is used to run docker images.

```
$ docker run php-app
```

```
root@irfan-G8-BXBT-2807:/home/irfan/Desktop/php-docker-app# docker run php-app
AH00558: apache2: Could not reliably determine the server's fully qualified domain name, using 172.17.0.2.
suppress this message
AH00558: apache2: Could not reliably determine the server's fully qualified domain name, using 172.17.0.2.
suppress this message
[Tue Apr 25 05:38:22.719813 2017] [mpm_prefork:notice] [pid 1] AH00163: Apache/2.4.10 (Debian) PHP/7.0.18
[Tue Apr 25 05:38:22.719885 2017] [core:notice] [pid 1] AH00094: Command line: 'apache2 -D FOREGROUND'
172.17.0.1 - - [25/Apr/2017:05:38:41 +0000] "GET / HTTP/1.1" 200 255 "-" "Mozilla/5.0 (X11; Ubuntu; Linux

172.17.0.1 - - [25/Apr/2017:05:38:41 +0000] "GET /favicon.ico HTTP/1.1" 404 501 "-" "Mozilla/5.0 (X11; Ubu
irefox/53.0"
172.17.0.1 - - [25/Apr/2017:05:38:42 +0000] "GET /favicon.ico HTTP/1.1" 404 501 "-" "Mozilla/5.0 (X11; Ubu
irefox/53.0"
172.17.0.1 - - [25/Apr/2017:05:38:47 +0000] "GET /favicon.ico HTTP/1.1" 404 502 "-" "Mozilla/5.0 (X11; Ubu
irefox/53.0"
```

We can see that our docker image is running and output is shown to the browser. This image is running on the 172.17.0.2 ip.

Output:

This is php file

Docker Python Application Example

To run python application in docker, we need to create Dockerfile. This application involves the following steps.

1. Create a directory.

```
$ cmd docker-python-app
```

```
root@irfan-GB-BXBT-2807: /home/docker
root@irfan-GB-BXBT-2807:/home/docker# mkdir python-docker-app
```

2. Enter into Directory

```
root@irfan-GB-BXBT-2807: /home/docker
root@irfan-GB-BXBT-2807:/home/docker# mkdir python-docker-app
root@irfan-GB-BXBT-2807:/home/docker# cd python-docker-app/
```

3. Create Dockerfile

It is require to create Docker image. It contains instructions that are read by Docker.

// Dockerfile

```
FROM python
COPY . /src
CMD ["python", "/src/index.py"]
```

4. Create a Python file

Create a python file to execute in the Docker container.

// index.py

```
print("Hello from python file");
```

5. Create Docker Image

To create Docker image of this python application, we need to use the following Docker command.

```
$ docker build -t python-app .
```

```
root@irfan-GB-BXBT-2807: /home/docker/python-docker-app
root@irfan-GB-BXBT-2807:/home/docker/python-docker-app# docker build -t python-app .
Sending build context to Docker daemon 3.072 kB
Step 1/3 : FROM python
latest: Pulling from library/python
cd0a524342ef: Pull complete
e39c3ffe4133: Pull complete
85334a7c2001: Pull complete
4c546d9d6a84: Pull complete
a2eb12d55dae: Pull complete
affc024c0a1b: Pull complete
08edbb62096c: Pull complete
Digest: sha256:a98a9d7e51321d2f440eb8b53b57e5121c7c1c325691ae0630466a12bf61d8db
Status: Downloaded newer image for python:latest
 ---> 92c4cfb9c80f
Step 2/3 : COPY . /src
 ---> 765e561988b1
Removing intermediate container 75f419044b13
Step 3/3 : CMD python /src/index.py
 ---> Running in dbb4cffa46f1
 ---> 098fdf099e67
Removing intermediate container dbb4cffa46f1
Successfully built 098fdf099e67
root@irfan-GB-BXBT-2807:/home/docker/python-docker-app# 
```

6. Check the available Docker images

We can see all the available Docker images by the following command.

```
$ docker images
```

```
root@irfan-GB-BXBT-2807: /home/docker/python-docker-app
root@irfan-GB-BXBT-2807:/home/docker/python-docker-app# docker images
REPOSITORY      TAG       IMAGE ID        CREATED            SIZE
python-app      latest    098fdf099e67    About a minute ago  689 MB
python          latest    92c4cfb9c80f    30 hours ago       689 MB
root@irfan-GB-BXBT-2807:/home/docker/python-docker-app# 
```

7. Run Docker

After creating docker image, now we can run it by using the following command.

```
$ docker run python-app
```

```
root@irfan-GB-BXBT-2807: /home/docker/python-docker-app
root@irfan-GB-BXBT-2807:/home/docker/python-docker-app# docker images
REPOSITORY          TAG          IMAGE ID          CREATED            SIZE
python-app          latest       098fdf099e67      About a minute ago 689 MB
python              latest       92c4cfb9c80f      30 hours ago       689 MB
root@irfan-GB-BXBT-2807:/home/docker/python-docker-app# docker run python-app
Hello from python file
root@irfan-GB-BXBT-2807:/home/docker/python-docker-app# █
```

The above command runs the Docker images and executes the python file. After executing, it produces the output which is shown in the above image.

Docker Scala Application Example

Docker allows us to execute Scala application. Here, we are creating a Scala file and executing that using the docker. This example includes the following steps.

1. Create a directory to organize application files.

```
$ mkdir scala-docker-app
```

```
root@irfan-GB-BXBT-2807: /home/docker
root@irfan-GB-BXBT-2807:/home/docker# mkdir scala-docker-app
```

2. Change working directory

```
$ cd scala-docker-app
```

```
root@irfan-GB-BXBT-2807: /home/docker/scala-docker-app
root@irfan-GB-BXBT-2807:/home/docker# mkdir scala-docker-app
root@irfan-GB-BXBT-2807:/home/docker# cd scala-docker-app/
root@irfan-GB-BXBT-2807:/home/docker/scala-docker-app#
```

3. Create a Dockerfile

// Dockerfile

```
FROM williamyeh/java7
MAINTAINER William Yeh <william.pjyeh@gmail.com>
ENV SCALA_VERSION 2.10.4
ENV SCALA_TARBALL http://www.scala-lang.org/files/archive/scala-$SCALA_VERSION.deb
RUN \
echo "==> Install curl helper tool..."&& \
```

```
apt-get update && \
DEBIAN_FRONTEND=noninteractive apt-get install -y --force-
yes curl && \
\
\
\
echo "===> install from Typesafe repo (contains old versions but th
ey have all dependencies we need later on)"&& \
curl -sSL http://apt.typesafe.com/repo-deb-build-0002.deb -
o repo-deb.deb && \
dpkg -i repo-deb.deb && \
apt-get update && \
\
\
\

echo "===> install Scala"&& \
DEBIAN_FRONTEND=noninteractive \
apt-get install -y --force-yes libjansi-java && \
curl -sSL $SCALA_TARBALL -o scala.deb && \
dpkg -i scala.deb && \
\
\
\
echo "===> clean up..."&& \
rm -f *.deb && \
apt-get remove -y --auto-remove curl && \
apt-get clean && \
rm -rf /var/lib/apt/lists/*
COPY . /root
WORKDIR /root
Run scalac index.scala
```

4. Create a Scala file

// index.scala

```scala
object MainObject{
def main(args:Array[String]){
println("Hello by Scala");
}
}
```

5. Create a Docker Image

Now, we are creating a Docker image of this Scala application. The following command is used to create Docker image.

```
$ docker build -t scala-app .
```

root@irfan-GB-BXBT-2807: /home/docker/scala-docker-app
root@irfan-GB-BXBT-2807:/home/docker/scala-docker-app# docker build -t scala-app .
Sending build context to Docker daemon 3.584 kB
Step 1/9 : FROM williamyeh/java7
latest: Pulling from williamyeh/java7
cd0a524342ef: Already exists
e76714c51132: Pull complete
Digest: sha256:596803ddbacfa6cd25a66b18cf2603f792dd11de66e3f539a162ff557068dda8
Status: Downloaded newer image for williamyeh/java7:latest
 ---> 23dbf232cb0e
Step 2/9 : MAINTAINER William Yeh <william.pjyeh@gmail.com>
 ---> Running in 64a0120404e9
 ---> c79e7028709a
Removing intermediate container 64a0120404e9
Step 3/9 : ENV SCALA_VERSION 2.10.4
 ---> Running in 49887a407453
 ---> 4f6c58aa364a
Removing intermediate container 49887a407453
Step 4/9 : ENV SCALA_TARBALL http://www.scala-lang.org/files/archive/scala-$SCALA_VERSION.deb
 ---> Running in f22a236fbbf0
 ---> 3f571e87dd3c
Removing intermediate container f22a236fbbf0
Step 5/9 : RUN echo "==> Install curl helper tool..." && apt-get update &&   DEBIAN_FRONTEND=non
cho "===> install from Typesafe repo (contains old versions but they have all dependencies we nee
po-deb-build-0002.deb -o repo-deb.deb && dpkg -i repo-deb.deb && apt-get update && echo "===>
t-get install -y --force-yes libjansi-java && curl -sSL $SCALA_TARBALL -o scala.deb && dpkg -i
 && apt-get remove -y --auto-remove curl &&   apt-get clean && rm -rf /var/lib/apt/lists/*
 ---> Running in f097783e0d10

6. Run Scala Docker image

```
$ docker run scala-app
```

```
root@irfan-GB-BXBT-2807:/home/docker/scala-docker-app
root@irfan-GB-BXBT-2807:/home/docker/scala-docker-app# docker run scala-app
Hello by Scala
root@irfan-GB-BXBT-2807:/home/docker/scala-docker-app# 
```

Docker Perl Application Example

In this example, we are creating a perl application and executing that using Docker. This example includes the following steps.

1. Create a directory to manage application files.

$ mkdir perl-docker-app

```
root@irfan-GB-BXBT-2807: /home/docker
File Edit View Search Terminal Help
root@irfan-GB-BXBT-2807:/home/docker# mkdir perl-docker-app
root@irfan-GB-BXBT-2807:/home/docker#
```

2. Change directory

$ cd perl-docker-app

```
root@irfan-GB-BXBT-2807: /home/docker/perl-docker-app
File Edit View Search Terminal Help
root@irfan-GB-BXBT-2807:/home/docker# mkdir perl-docker-app
root@irfan-GB-BXBT-2807:/home/docker# cd perl-docker-app/
root@irfan-GB-BXBT-2807:/home/docker/perl-docker-app#
```

3. Create a Docker file

// Dockerfile

```
FROM perl:5.20
COPY . /var/www/php
WORKDIR /var/www/php
CMD [ "perl", "index.pl"]
```

4. Create a Perl file

// index.pl

```perl
print "Hello from perl file";
```

5. Create Docker Image

```
$ docker build -t perl-app .
```

```
root@irfan-GB-BXBT-2807: /home/docker/perl-docker-app
File Edit View Search Terminal Help
root@irfan-GB-BXBT-2807:/home/docker/perl-docker-app# docker build -t perl-app .
Sending build context to Docker daemon 3.072 kB
Step 1/4 : FROM perl:5.20
5.20: Pulling from library/perl
8b87079b7a06: Pull complete
a3ed95caeb02: Pull complete
1bb8eaf3d643: Pull complete
3e04171ce2e5: Pull complete
0b73d3fea769: Pull complete
ffb34b57cdf2: Pull complete
8eeaf71aee14: Pull complete
72cfc9cbff48: Pull complete
2d693787a8c5: Pull complete
Digest: sha256:5e06bbcf01ed88d6812839bcc7645a3960361a6843e14b6337de2897dfb2863f
Status: Downloaded newer image for perl:5.20
 ---> bbe5a82c1dbe
Step 2/4 : COPY . /var/www/html
 ---> 58059b3af315
Removing intermediate container 522a020b98d7
Step 3/4 : WORKDIR /var/www/html
 ---> 1589c359dc7b
Removing intermediate container d5a4aafb1219
Step 4/4 : CMD perl index.pl
 ---> Running in 0e910453461f
 ---> e1e4e4b5acf9
Removing intermediate container 0e910453461f
Successfully built e1e4e4b5acf9
root@irfan-GB-BXBT-2807:/home/docker/perl-docker-app#
```

6. Run the build image

```
$ docker run perl-app
```

```
root@irfan-GB-BXBT-2807:/home/docker/perl-docker-app# docker run perl-app
Hello from perl file
root@irfan-GB-BXBT-2807:/home/docker/perl-docker-app#
```

After running the docker image it executes the perl script and print a message in the console screen.

Docker Ruby Application Example

In the following example, we are creating a ruby script file which run by using Docker. It consists of the following steps:

1. Create a directory to organize application files

```
$ mkdir ruby-docker-app
```

```
● ● ●   root@irfan-GB-BXBT-2807: /home/docker
File  Edit  View  Search  Terminal  Help
root@irfan-GB-BXBT-2807:/home/docker# mkdir ruby-docker-app
root@irfan-GB-BXBT-2807:/home/docker# █
```

2. Change Directory

```
$ cd ruby-docker-app
```

```
● ● ●   root@irfan-GB-BXBT-2807: /home/docker/ruby-docker-app
File  Edit  View  Search  Terminal  Help
root@irfan-GB-BXBT-2807:/home/docker# mkdir ruby-docker-app
root@irfan-GB-BXBT-2807:/home/docker# cd ruby-docker-app/
root@irfan-GB-BXBT-2807:/home/docker/ruby-docker-app# █
```

3. Create a Dockerfile

Dockerfile is used to contain instructions for the docker.

// Dockerfile

```
FROM ruby:2
COPY . /var/www/ruby
WORKDIR /var/www/ruby
CMD ["ruby","index.rb"]
```

4. Create a ruby file

// index.rb

```
puts "Hello from ruby!";
```

5. Create Docker Image

```
$ docker build -t ruby-app .
```

```
root@irfan-GB-BXBT-2807: /home/docker/ruby-docker-app
File Edit View Search Terminal Help
root@irfan-GB-BXBT-2807:/home/docker/ruby-docker-app# docker build -t ruby-app .
Sending build context to Docker daemon 3.072 kB
Step 1/4 : FROM ruby:2
2: Pulling from library/ruby
cd0a524342ef: Already exists
e39c3ffe4133: Already exists
85334a7c2001: Already exists
4c546d9d6a84: Already exists
dd2ea17fcd18: Pull complete
234e7744cd9b: Pull complete
dcbfbb4bf16f: Pull complete
97488e0bf2cc: Pull complete
Digest: sha256:318ab2923172c6ad851c43285a9b2772a417801b7cdafc770f72e726d4846055
Status: Downloaded newer image for ruby:2
 ---> 03f5d188b6ac
Step 2/4 : COPY . /var/www/html
 ---> ed4ee6edaf42
Removing intermediate container 9cf48e5b9bca
Step 3/4 : WORKDIR /var/www/html
 ---> 445058a98dd8
Removing intermediate container 6dcb9ef4dc3b
Step 4/4 : CMD ruby index.rb
 ---> Running in 39d7b81bb738
 ---> 21c624bbf791
Removing intermediate container 39d7b81bb738
Successfully built 21c624bbf791
root@irfan-GB-BXBT-2807:/home/docker/ruby-docker-app#
```

6. Run the Docker Image

```
$ docker run ruby-app
```

```
root@irfan-GB-BXBT-2807:/home/docker/ruby-docker-app# docker run ruby-app
Hello from ruby!
root@irfan-GB-BXBT-2807:/home/docker/ruby-docker-app#
```

In the above image, we can see that ruby script has been executed and prints the output on the console.

Docker Swift Application Example

Docker allows us to execute swift application. In the following example, we are creating a swift file which run by using Docker. It consists of the following steps:

1. Create a directory to organize application files.

```
$ mkdir swift-docker-app
```

```
⊗ ⊖ ⊙   root@irfan-GB-BXBT-2807: /home/docker
File Edit View Search Terminal Help
root@irfan-GB-BXBT-2807:/home/docker# mkdir swift-docker-app
root@irfan-GB-BXBT-2807:/home/docker# ▊
```

2. Change Directory

```
$ cd swift-docker-app
```

```
⊗ ⊖ ⊙   root@irfan-GB-BXBT-2807: /home/docker/swift-docker-app
File Edit View Search Terminal Help
root@irfan-GB-BXBT-2807:/home/docker# mkdir swift-docker-app
root@irfan-GB-BXBT-2807:/home/docker# cd swift-docker-app/
root@irfan-GB-BXBT-2807:/home/docker/swift-docker-app# ▊
```

3. Create a Dockerfile

It is required to contains necessary Docker instructions which are used by Docker to create image.

// Dockerfile

```
FROM ubuntu:16.04

MAINTAINER Haris Amin <aminharis7@gmail.com>
```

```
# Install related packages and set LLVM 3.6 as the compile
r
RUN apt-get -q update && \
apt-get -q install -y \
make \
libc6-dev \
clang-3.6 \
curl \
libedit-dev \
python2.7 \
python2.7-dev \
libicu-dev \
rsync \
libxml2 \
git \
libcurl4-openssl-dev \
&& update-alternatives --quiet --
install /usr/bin/clang clang /usr/bin/clang-3.6 100 \
&& update-alternatives --quiet --
install /usr/bin/clang++ clang++ /usr/bin/clang++-
3.6 100 \
&& rm -r /var/lib/apt/lists/*
# Everything up to here should cache nicely between Swift
versions, assuming dev dependencies change little
ENV SWIFT_BRANCH=swift-3.0.2-release \
SWIFT_VERSION=swift-3.0.2-RELEASE \
SWIFT_PLATFORM=ubuntu16.04 \
PATH=/usr/bin:$PATH
# Download GPG keys, signature and Swift package, then unp
ack and cleanup
RUN SWIFT_URL=https://swift.org/builds/$SWIFT_BRANCH/$(echo "
$SWIFT_PLATFORM" | tr -d .)/$SWIFT_VERSION/$SWIFT_VERSION-
$SWIFT_PLATFORM.tar.gz \
```

```
&& curl -fSsL $SWIFT_URL -o swift.tar.gz \
&& curl -fSsL $SWIFT_URL.sig -o swift.tar.gz.sig \
&& export GNUPGHOME="$(mktemp -d)" \
&& set -e; \
for key in \
# pub    4096R/412B37AD 2015-11-19 [expires: 2017-11-18]
#        Key fingerprint = 7463 A81A 4B2E EA1B 551F  FBCF
D441 C977 412B 37AD
# uid                  Swift Automatic Signing Key #1 <swi
ft-infrastructure@swift.org>
7463A81A4B2EEA1B551FFBCFD441C977412B37AD \
# pub    4096R/21A56D5F 2015-11-28 [expires: 2017-11-27]
#        Key fingerprint = 1BE1 E29A 084C B305 F397  D62A 9
F59 7F4D 21A5 6D5F
# uid                  Swift 2.2 Release Signing Key <swif
t-infrastructure@swift.org>
1BE1E29A084CB305F397D62A9F597F4D21A56D5F \
# pub    4096R/91D306C6 2016-05-31 [expires: 2018-05-31]
#        Key fingerprint = A3BA FD35 56A5 9079 C068  94BD
63BC 1CFE 91D3 06C6
# uid                  Swift 3.x Release Signing Key <swif
t-infrastructure@swift.org>
A3BAFD3556A59079C06894BD63BC1CFE91D306C6 \
; do \
gpg --quiet --keyserver ha.pool.sks-keyservers.net --recv-
keys "$key"; \
done \
&& gpg --batch --verify --
quiet swift.tar.gz.sig swift.tar.gz \
&& tar -xzf swift.tar.gz --directory / --strip-
components=1 \
&& rm -r "$GNUPGHOME" swift.tar.gz.sig swift.tar.gz
```

```
# Print Installed Swift Version
RUN swift --version
COPY . /var/www/java
WORKDIR /var/www/java
CMD ["swift","index.swift"]
```

4. Create a swift file

Afetr creating a Dockerfile, we are creating a Swift file. This includes only one print statement that will produce the output when Docker images is run.

// index.swift

```
print("Hello from swift")
```

5. Create Docker Image

Now. Follow the following command to build Docker image.

```
$ docker build -t swift-app .
```

```
●●●  root@irfan-GB-BXBT-2807: /home/docker/swift-docker-app
File Edit View Search Terminal Help
root@irfan-GB-BXBT-2807:/home/docker/swift-docker-app# docker build -t swift-app .
Sending build context to Docker daemon  5.12 kB
Step 1/9 : FROM ubuntu:16.04
16.04: Pulling from library/ubuntu
aafe6b5e13de: Pull complete
0a2b43a72660: Pull complete
18bdd1e546d2: Pull complete
8198342c3e05: Pull complete
f56970a44fd4: Pull complete
Digest: sha256:f3a61450ae43896c4332bda5e78b453f4a93179045f20c8181043b26b5e79028
Status: Downloaded newer image for ubuntu:16.04
 ---> f7b3f317ec73
Step 2/9 : MAINTAINER Haris Amin <aminharis7@gmail.com>
 ---> Running in 630d8a8e089e
 ---> 3ce011562443
Removing intermediate container 630d8a8e089e
Step 3/9 : RUN apt-get -q update &&      apt-get -q install -y      make      libc6-d
ev      clang-3.6      curl      libedit-dev      python2.7      python2.7-dev      libi
cu-dev      rsync      libxml2      git      libcurl4-openssl-dev      && update-altern
atives --quiet --install /usr/bin/clang clang /usr/bin/clang-3.6 100      && update
-alternatives --quiet --install /usr/bin/clang++ clang++ /usr/bin/clang++-3.6 100
    && rm -r /var/lib/apt/lists/*
 ---> Running in ebc37dd947b3
```

6. Running the Docker Image

$ docker run swift-app

```
root@irfan-GB-BXBT-2807: /home/docker/swift-docker-app
File Edit View Search Terminal Help
 ---> 752501cc6013
Removing intermediate container 5406380c5145
Step 6/9 : RUN swift --version
 ---> Running in 4d78927de736
Swift version 3.0.2 (swift-3.0.2-RELEASE)
Target: x86_64-unknown-linux-gnu
 ---> a6b81e2ba7f0
Removing intermediate container 4d78927de736
Step 7/9 : COPY . /var/www/html
 ---> bdfe70200d33
Removing intermediate container 868247bc7c6d
Step 8/9 : WORKDIR /var/www/html
 ---> 078ed3dbe24e
Removing intermediate container 0b609d93dcc8
Step 9/9 : CMD swift index.swift
 ---> Running in 63d178c841c9
 ---> e88107e7a016
Removing intermediate container 63d178c841c9
Successfully built e88107e7a016
root@irfan-GB-BXBT-2807:/home/docker/swift-docker-app# docker run swift-app
Hello from swift
root@irfan-GB-BXBT-2807:/home/docker/swift-docker-app#
```

Docker Ubuntu Example

Docker also allows us to install any operating system in isolated container. Here, in the following example, we are installing Ubuntu in Docker.

1. Create a directory to organize files.

```
$ mkdir ubuntu-in-docker
```

```
⊗ ⊝ ⊜   root@irfan-GB-BXBT-2807: /home/docker
File Edit View Search Terminal Help
root@irfan-GB-BXBT-2807:/home/docker# mkdir ubuntu-in-docker
root@irfan-GB-BXBT-2807:/home/docker# █
```

2. Change the directory

```
$ cd ubuntu-in-docker
```

```
⊗ ⊝ ⊜   root@irfan-GB-BXBT-2807: /home/docker/ubuntu-in-docker
File Edit View Search Terminal Help
root@irfan-GB-BXBT-2807:/home/docker# mkdir ubuntu-in-docker
root@irfan-GB-BXBT-2807:/home/docker# cd ubuntu-in-docker/
root@irfan-GB-BXBT-2807:/home/docker/ubuntu-in-docker# █
```

3. Create Dockerfile

In the file, we are using only one instruction that will pull the Ubuntu image from Docker hub.

// Dockerfile

```
FROM ubuntu
```

4. Create a Docker Image

```
$ docker build -t ubuntu-in-doker .
```

```
root@irfan-GB-BXBT-2807: /home/docker/ubuntu-in-docker
root@irfan-GB-BXBT-2807:/home/docker/ubuntu-in-docker# docker build -t ubuntu-os .
Sending build context to Docker daemon 2.048 kB
Step 1/1 : FROM ubuntu
latest: Pulling from library/ubuntu
Digest: sha256:f3a61450ae43896c4332bda5e78b453f4a93179045f20c8181043b26b5e79028
Status: Downloaded newer image for ubuntu:latest
 ---> f7b3f317ec73
Successfully built f7b3f317ec73
root@irfan-GB-BXBT-2807:/home/docker/ubuntu-in-docker#
```

5. Run Docker Image

The image, we have created is run by the following command.

```
$ docker run -td ubuntu-os
```

```
root@irfan-GB-BXBT-2807: /home/docker/ubuntu-in-docker
root@irfan-GB-BXBT-2807:/home/docker/ubuntu-in-docker# docker run -td ubuntu-os
a2e21af03a95284e56aad2cac96eaf296f4228091802303224e013ae9e729d6e
root@irfan-GB-BXBT-2807:/home/docker/ubuntu-in-docker#
```

6. See Running Container

This command is used to see the all running Docker container.

```
$ docker ps -a
```

```
root@irfan-GB-BXBT-2807: /home/docker/ubuntu-in-docker
root@irfan-GB-BXBT-2807:/home/docker/ubuntu-in-docker# docker ps -a
CONTAINER ID      IMAGE         COMMAND           CREATED         STATUS
a2e21af03a95      ubuntu-os     "/bin/bash"       6 minutes ago   Up 6 minutes
root@irfan-GB-BXBT-2807:/home/docker/ubuntu-in-docker#
```

7. Enter into Docker Container

We can enter into the running container and can check the files and application inside the container.

```
$ docker exec -it a2e21af03a95 bash
```

```
root@a2e21af03a95:/
root@irfan-GB-BXBT-2807:/home/docker/ubuntu-in-docker# docker ps -a
CONTAINER ID      IMAGE        COMMAND        CREATED        STATUS
a2e21af03a95      ubuntu-os    "/bin/bash"    6 minutes ago  Up 6 minutes
root@irfan-GB-BXBT-2807:/home/docker/ubuntu-in-docker# docker exec -it a2e21af03a95 bash
root@a2e21af03a95:/#
```

8. See Ubuntu OS Directory Structure

After entering into

```
root@a2e21af03a95:/
root@irfan-GB-BXBT-2807:/home/docker/ubuntu-in-docker# docker ps -a
CONTAINER ID      IMAGE        COMMAND        CREATED        STATUS          PO
a2e21af03a95      ubuntu-os    "/bin/bash"    6 minutes ago  Up 6 minutes
root@irfan-GB-BXBT-2807:/home/docker/ubuntu-in-docker# docker exec -it a2e21af03a95 bash
root@a2e21af03a95:/# ls
bin  boot  dev  etc  home  lib  lib64  media  mnt  opt  proc  root  run  sbin  srv  sys  tmp  usr  var
root@a2e21af03a95:/#
```

9. Executing Commands

```
$ apt-get update
```

```
root@a2e21af03a95:/
root@irfan-GB-BXBT-2807:/home/docker/ubuntu-in-docker# docker ps -a
CONTAINER ID      IMAGE        COMMAND        CREATED        STATUS
a2e21af03a95      ubuntu-os    "/bin/bash"    6 minutes ago  Up 6 minutes
root@irfan-GB-BXBT-2807:/home/docker/ubuntu-in-docker# docker exec -it a2e21af03a95 bash
root@a2e21af03a95:/# ls
bin  boot  dev  etc  home  lib  lib64  media  mnt  opt  proc  root  run  sbin  srv  sys  tmp
root@a2e21af03a95:/# apt-get update
Get:1 http://security.ubuntu.com/ubuntu xenial-security InRelease [102 kB]
Get:2 http://archive.ubuntu.com/ubuntu xenial InRelease [247 kB]
Get:3 http://security.ubuntu.com/ubuntu xenial-security/universe Sources [30.3 kB]
Get:4 http://archive.ubuntu.com/ubuntu xenial-updates InRelease [102 kB]
Get:5 http://security.ubuntu.com/ubuntu xenial-security/main amd64 Packages [320 kB]
Get:6 http://archive.ubuntu.com/ubuntu xenial-backports InRelease [102 kB]
Get:7 http://security.ubuntu.com/ubuntu xenial-security/restricted amd64 Packages [12.8 kB]
Get:8 http://security.ubuntu.com/ubuntu xenial-security/universe amd64 Packages [135 kB]
Get:9 http://archive.ubuntu.com/ubuntu xenial/universe Sources [9802 kB]
Get:10 http://security.ubuntu.com/ubuntu xenial-security/multiverse amd64 Packages [2936 B]
Get:11 http://archive.ubuntu.com/ubuntu xenial/main amd64 Packages [1558 kB]
Get:12 http://archive.ubuntu.com/ubuntu xenial/restricted amd64 Packages [14.1 kB]
Get:13 http://archive.ubuntu.com/ubuntu xenial/universe amd64 Packages [9827 kB]
84% [13 Packages 8104 kB/9827 kB 82%]
```

Docker Push Repository

We can push our Docker image to global repository. It is a public repository provided by Docker officially. It allows us to put our docker image on the server. It is helpful when we want to access our docker image from global. Follow the following steps to push custom image on the Docker hub.

1. login to hub.docker.com

We need to login to our account of Docker hub. If you don't have, create it first.

```
$ docker login
```

```
root@irfan-GB-BXBT-2807: /
root@irfan-GB-BXBT-2807:/# docker login
Login with your Docker ID to push and pull images from Docker Hub. If you don't
have a Docker ID, head over to https://hub.docker.com to create one.
Username:
```

It will ask for username. Enter the dockerid here and press enter.

```
root@irfan-GB-BXBT-2807: /
root@irfan-GB-BXBT-2807:/# docker login
Login with your Docker ID to push and pull images from Docker Hub. If you don't
have a Docker ID, head over to https://hub.docker.com to create one.
Username: dockerid4irfan
Password:
Login Succeeded
root@irfan-GB-BXBT-2807:/#
```

After providing username, it asks for password. Enter your account password here and it will show you your login status as succeeded.

2. Tag Docker Image

After login, we need to tag our docker image that we want to push. Following command is used to tag the docker image.

```
$ docker tag image-name username/image-name
```

username refers to our dockerid or the username which is used to login.

image-name is the name of our docker image present on our system.

See, screen shot of the above command.

```
root@irfan-GB-BXBT-2807:/home/irfan
root@irfan-GB-BXBT-2807:/home/irfan# docker tag hello-world dockerid4irfan/hello-world
root@irfan-GB-BXBT-2807:/home/irfan# █
```

In the above command, we have tagged docker image *hello-world*. Now, we need to push it to the repository. Let?s see it in the below command.

3. Push Docker Image

The following command is used to push docker image to docker hub repository.

```
$ docker push   username/image-name
```

See, screen shot of the above command.

```
root@irfan-GB-BXBT-2807:/home/irfan
root@irfan-GB-BXBT-2807:/home/irfan# docker tag hello-world dockerid4irfan/hello-world
root@irfan-GB-BXBT-2807:/home/irfan# docker push dockerid4irfan/hello-world
The push refers to a repository [docker.io/dockerid4irfan/hello-world]
98c944e98de8: Mounted from library/hello-world
latest: digest: sha256:c5515758d4c5e1e838e9cd307f6c6a0d620b5e07e6f927b07d05f6d12a1ac8d
7 size: 524
root@irfan-GB-BXBT-2807:/home/irfan# █
```

In the above screen shot, we can see that docker image has been pushed successfully.

Now, login into our account at hub.docker.com and check our dashboard. It will have a new docker image named *dockerid4irfan/hello-world.*

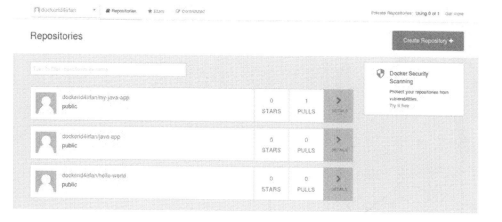

Look at the screen shot, it has the newest one docker image which is just pushed. On the top, the first one is the newest image.

Docker Useful Commands

Docker is natively Linux based software so that it provides commands to interact and work in the client-server environment.

Here, we have listed some important and useful Docker commands.

Check Docker version

$ docker version

It shows docker version for both client and server. As given in the following image.

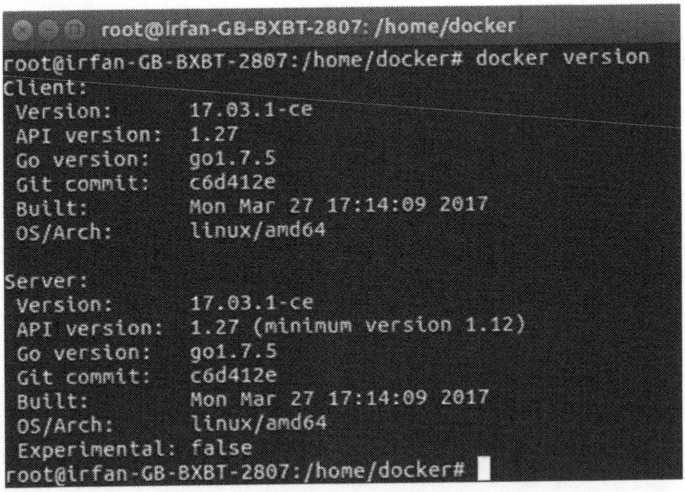

```
root@irfan-GB-BXBT-2807: /home/docker
root@irfan-GB-BXBT-2807:/home/docker# docker version
Client:
 Version:      17.03.1-ce
 API version:  1.27
 Go version:   go1.7.5
 Git commit:   c6d412e
 Built:        Mon Mar 27 17:14:09 2017
 OS/Arch:      linux/amd64

Server:
 Version:      17.03.1-ce
 API version:  1.27 (minimum version 1.12)
 Go version:   go1.7.5
 Git commit:   c6d412e
 Built:        Mon Mar 27 17:14:09 2017
 OS/Arch:      linux/amd64
 Experimental: false
root@irfan-GB-BXBT-2807:/home/docker#
```

Build Docker Image from a Dockerfile

$ docker build -t image-name docker-file-location

-t : it is used to tag Docker image with the provided name.

Run Docker Image

```
$ docker run -d image-name
```

-d : It is used to create a daemon process.

Check available Docker images

```
$ docker images
```

Check for latest running container

```
$ docker ps -l
```

-l : it is used to show latest available container.

Check all running containers

```
$ docker ps -a
```

-a : It is used to show all available containers.

Stop running container

```
$ docker stop container_id
```

container_id : It is an Id assigned by the Docker to the container.

Delete an image

```
$ docker rmi image-name
```

Delete all images

```
$ docker rmi $(docker images -q)
```

Delete all images forcefully

```
$ docker rmi -r $(docker images -q)
```

-r : It is used to delete image forcefully.

Delete all containers

```
$ docker rm $(docker ps -a -q)
```

Enter into Docker container

```
$ docker exec -it container-id bash
```

Docker Cloud

Docker provides us the facility to store and fetch docker images on the cloud registry. We can store dockerized images either privately or publicly. It is a full GUI interface that allows us to manage builds, images, swarms, nodes and apps.

The Docker Cloud is a service provided by Docker in which you can carry out the following operations –

❖ Nodes – You can connect the Docker Cloud to your existing cloud providers such as Azure and AWS to spin up containers on these environments.
❖ Cloud Repository – Provides a place where you can store your own repositories.
❖ Continuous Integration – Connect with Github and build a continuous integration pipeline.
❖ Application Deployment – Deploy and scale infrastructure and containers.
❖ Continuous Deployment – Can automate deployments.

Getting started

You can go to the following link to getting started with Docker Cloud – https://cloud.docker.com/

We need to have Docker ID to access and control images. If we don't have, create it first.

Here, in the following screenshot, we have logged in to Docker cloud. It shows a welcome page.

In the left panel, we can see that it provides lots of functionalities that we use on the cloud. Apart from all these, let's create a repository first.

Creating Repository

To create Docker cloud repository, click on the create repository +button available on the welcome page at the bottom.

After clicking, it displays a form to enter the name of the repository. The page looks looks like the following.

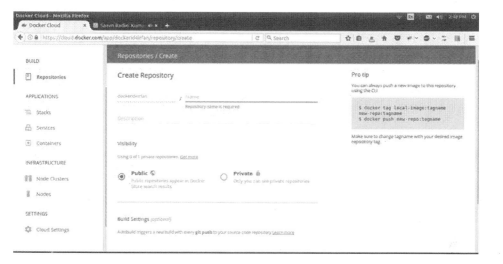

It asks for the repository name to create a new one. The following screen-shot show the description.

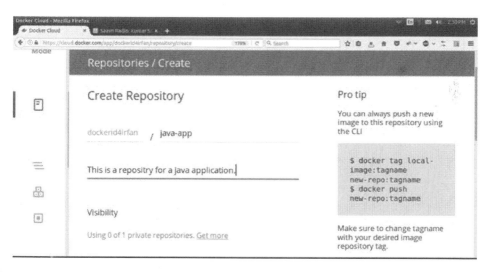

After filling the details, we should make this repository public. Now, just click on the create button at the bottom. It will create repository for us.

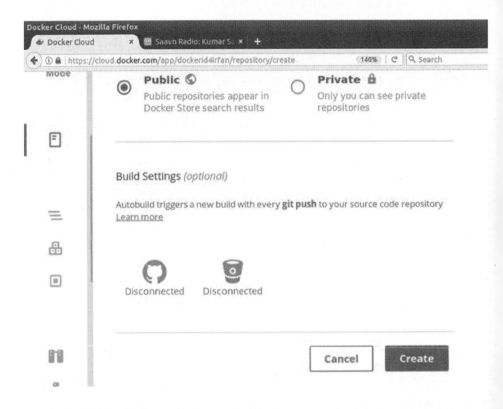

So, we can see that it provides the other tools also to manage and control Docker cloud.

Connecting to the Cloud Provider

The first step is to connect to an existing cloud provider. The following steps will show you how to connect with an Amazon Cloud provider.

Step 1 − The first step is to ensure that you have the right AWS keys. This can be taken from the aws console. Log into your aws account using the following link − https://aws.amazon.com/console/

Step 2 − Once logged in, go to the Security Credentials section. Make a note of the access keys which will be used from Docker Hub.

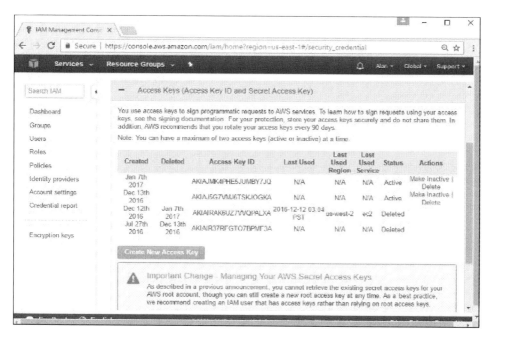

Step 3 – Next, you need to create a policy in aws that will allow Docker to view EC2 instances. Go to the profiles section in aws. Click the Create Policy button.

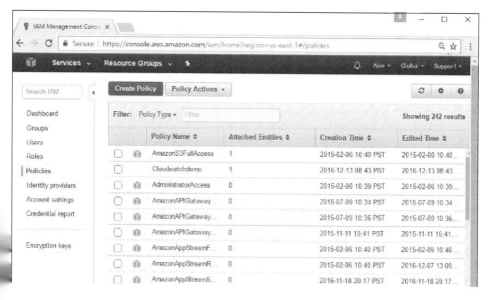

Step 4 – Click on 'Create Your Own Policy' and give the policy name as dockercloudpolicy and the policy definition as shown below.

```
{
    "Version": "2012-10-17",
    "Statement": [ {
        "Action": [
            "ec2:*",
            "iam:ListInstanceProfiles"
        ],
        "Effect": "Allow",
        "Resource": "*"
    } ]
}
```

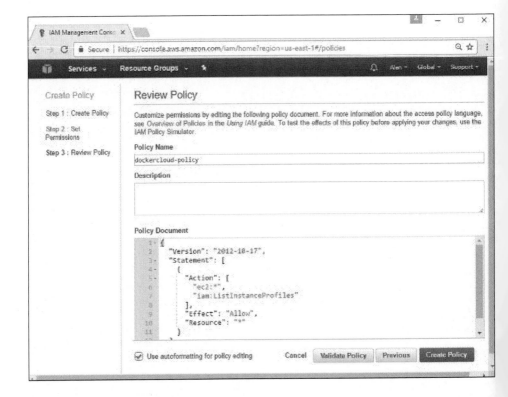

Next, click the Create Policy button

Step 5 – Next, you need to create a role which will be used by Docker to spin up nodes on AWS. For this, go to the Roles section in AWS and click the Create New Role option.

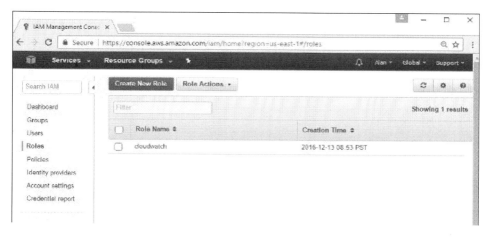

Step 6 – Give the name for the role as dockercloud-role.

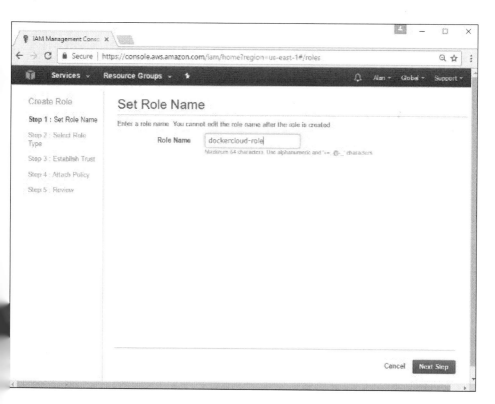

Step 7 – On the next screen, go to 'Role for Cross Account Access' and select "Provide access between your account and a 3rd party AWS account".

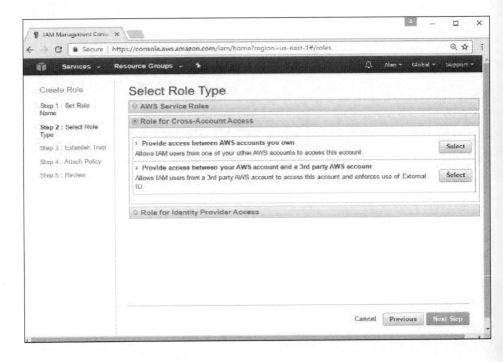

Step 8 – On the next screen, enter the following details –

❖ In the Account ID field, enter the ID for the Docker Cloud service: 689684103426.
❖ In the External ID field, enter your Docker Cloud username.

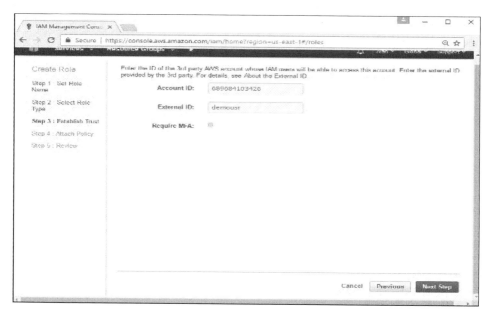

Step 9 – Then, click the Next Step button and on the next screen, attach the policy which was created in the earlier step.

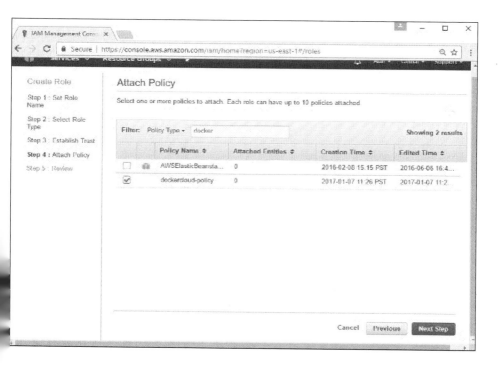

Step 10 – Finally, on the last screen when the role is created, make sure to copy the arn role which is created.

```
arn:aws:iam::085363624145:role/dockercloud-role
```

Step 11 – Now go back to Docker Cloud, select Cloud Providers, and click the plug symbol next to Amazon Web Services.

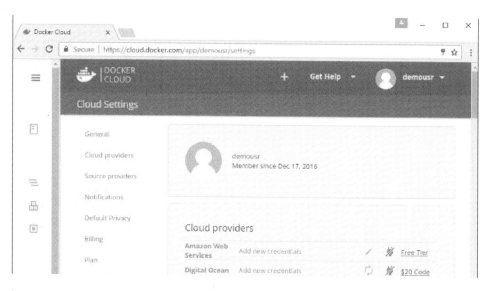

Enter the arn role and click the Save button.

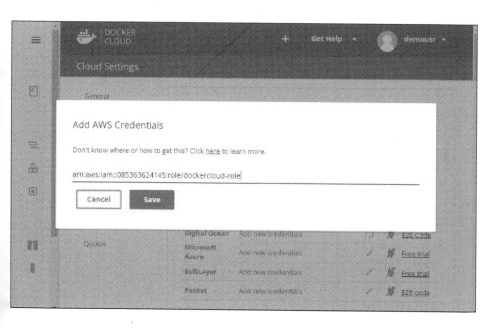

Once saved, the integration with AWS would be complete.

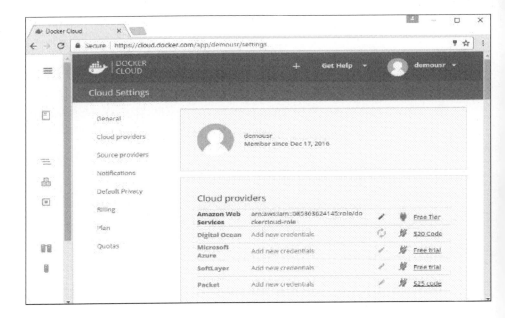

Setting Up Nodes

Once the integration with AWS is complete, the next step is to setup a node. Go to the Nodes section in Docker Cloud. Note that the setting up of nodes will automatically setup a node cluster first.

Step 1 – Go to the Nodes section in Docker Cloud.

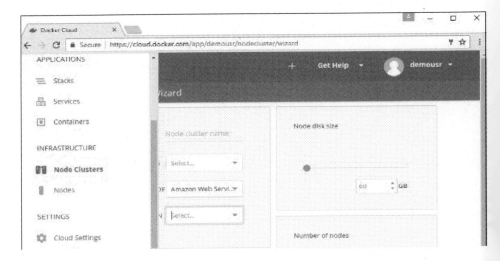

Step 2 – Next, you can give the details of the nodes which will be setup in AWS.

You can then click the Launch Node cluster which will be present at the bottom of the screen. Once the node is deployed, you will get the notification in the Node Cluster screen.

Deploying a Service

The next step after deploying a node is to deploy a service. To do this, we need to perform the following steps.

Step 1 – Go to the Services Section in Docker Cloud. Click the Create button

Step 2 – Choose the Service which is required. In our case, let's choose mongo.

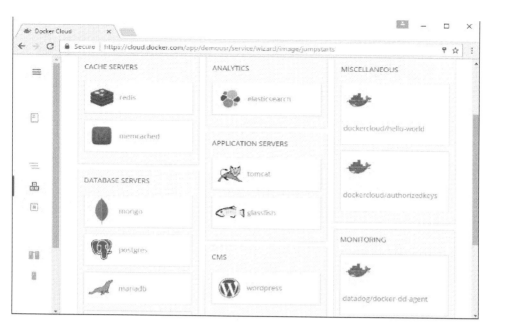

Step 3 — On the next screen, choose the Create & Deploy option. This will start deploying the Mongo container on your node cluster.

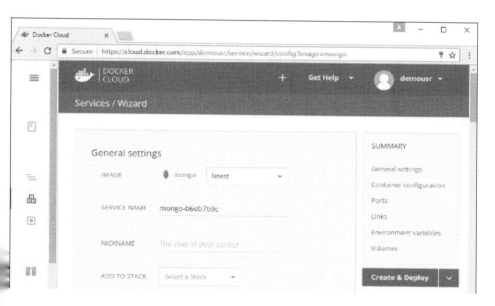

Once deployed, you will be able to see the container in a running state.

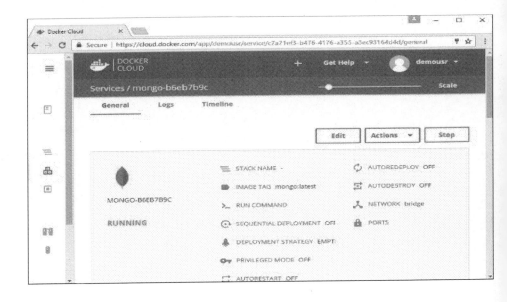

Docker Compose

It is a tool which is used to create and start Docker application by using a single command. We can use it to file to configure our application's services.

It is a great tool for development, testing, and staging environments.

It provides the following commands for managing the whole lifecycle of our application.

- ❖ Start, stop and rebuild services
- ❖ View the status of running services
- ❖ Stream the log output of running services
- ❖ Run a one-off command on a service

To implement compose, it consists the following steps.

1. Put Application environment variables inside the Dockerfile to access publicly.
2. Provide services name in the docker-compose.yml file so they can be run together in an isolated environment.
3. run docker-compose up and Compose will start and run your entire app.

A typical docker-compose.yml file has the following format and arguments.

// docker-compose.yml

```
version: '3'
services:
web:
build: .
ports:
- "5000:5000"
volumes:
- .:/code
- logvolume01:/var/log
```

```
links:
- redis
redis:
image: redis
volumes:
logvolume01: {}
```

Installing Docker Compose

Following are the instructions to install Docker Compose in Linux Ubuntu.

```
curl -
L https://github.com/docker/compose/releases/download/1.1
2.0/docker-compose-`uname -s`-`uname -
m` > /usr/local/bin/docker-compose
```

Docker-compose version

```
$ docker-compose --version
```

It says, permission denied. So, make file executable.

```
$ sudo chmod +x /usr/local/bin/docker-compose
```

```
root@irfan-GB-BXBT-2807: /home/irfan
root@irfan-GB-BXBT-2807:/home/irfan# docker-compose version
bash: /usr/local/bin/docker-compose: Permission denied
root@irfan-GB-BXBT-2807:/home/irfan# sudo chmod +x /usr/local/bin/docker-compose
root@irfan-GB-BXBT-2807:/home/irfan#
```

Now, check version again.

```
$ docker-compose ?version
```

```
root@irfan-GB-BXBT-2807: /home/irfan
root@irfan-GB-BXBT-2807:/home/irfan# docker-compose version
bash: /usr/local/bin/docker-compose: Permission denied
root@irfan-GB-BXBT-2807:/home/irfan# sudo chmod +x /usr/local/bin/docker-compose
root@irfan-GB-BXBT-2807:/home/irfan# docker-compose --version
docker-compose version 1.12.0, build b31ff33
root@irfan-GB-BXBT-2807:/home/irfan#
```

Running Application using Docker Compose

Example

Follow the following example

1. Create a Directory

```
$ mkdir docker-compose-example
$ cd docker-composer-example
```

2) Create a file app.py.

// app.py

```python
from flask import Flask
from redis import Redis
app = Flask(__name__)
redis = Redis(host='redis', port=6379)
@app.route('/')
def hello():
count = redis.incr('hits')
return 'Hello World! I have been seen {} times.\n'.format(
count)
```

```
if __name__ == "__main__":
app.run(host="0.0.0.0", debug=True)
```

3) Create a file requirements.txt.

// requirements.txt

```
flask
redis
```

4) Create a Dockerfile.

// Dockerfile

```
FROM python:3.4-alpine
ADD . /code
WORKDIR /code
RUN pip install -r requirements.txt
CMD ["python", "app.py"]
5) Create a Compose File.
```

// docker-compose.yml

```
version: '2'
services:
web:
build: .
ports:
- "5000:5000"
volumes:
- .:/code
redis:
image: "redis:alpine"
```

6) Build and Run Docker App with Compose

```
$ docker-compose up
```

After running the above command, it shows the following output.

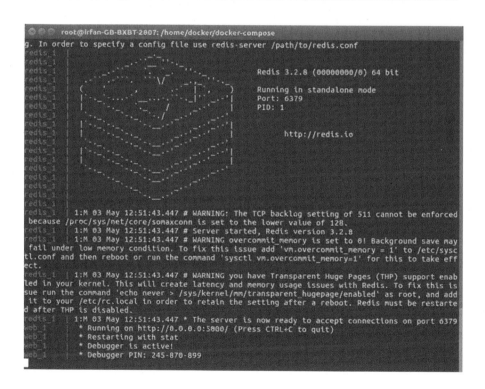

```
root@irfan-GB-BXBT-2807: /home/docker/docker-compose
root@irfan-GB-BXBT-2807:/home/docker/docker-compose# docker-compose up
Creating network "dockercompose_default" with the default driver
Building web
Step 1/5 : FROM python:3.4-alpine
 ---> f9b5ec164bb9
Step 2/5 : ADD . /code
 ---> ce7a951b7838
Removing intermediate container 98e19cab51a2
Step 3/5 : WORKDIR /code
 ---> 71e481420282
Removing intermediate container 20e81ef49e15
Step 4/5 : RUN pip install -r requirements.txt
 ---> Running in 278db10fa751
Collecting flask (from -r requirements.txt (line 1))
  Downloading Flask-0.12.1-py2.py3-none-any.whl (82kB)
Collecting redis (from -r requirements.txt (line 2))
  Downloading redis-2.10.5-py2.py3-none-any.whl (60kB)
Collecting Jinja2>=2.4 (from flask->-r requirements.txt (line 1))
  Downloading Jinja2-2.9.6-py2.py3-none-any.whl (340kB)
Collecting click>=2.0 (from flask->-r requirements.txt (line 1))
  Downloading click-6.7-py2.py3-none-any.whl (71kB)
Collecting Werkzeug>=0.7 (from flask->-r requirements.txt (line 1))
  Downloading Werkzeug-0.12.1-py2.py3-none-any.whl (312kB)
Collecting itsdangerous>=0.21 (from flask->-r requirements.txt (line 1))
  Downloading itsdangerous-0.24.tar.gz (46kB)
Collecting MarkupSafe>=0.23 (from Jinja2>=2.4->flask->-r requirements.txt (line 1))
  Downloading MarkupSafe-1.0.tar.gz
Building wheels for collected packages: itsdangerous, MarkupSafe
  Running setup.py bdist_wheel for itsdangerous: started
  Running setup.py bdist_wheel for itsdangerous: finished with status 'done'
  Stored in directory: /root/.cache/pip/wheels/fc/a8/66/24d655233c757e178d45dea2de22a04c6d92766
```

```
root@irfan-GB-BXBT-2807: /home/docker/docker-compose
g. In order to specify a config file use redis-server /path/to/redis.conf
redis_1  |
redis_1  |                                           Redis 3.2.8 (00000000/0) 64 bit
redis_1  |                                           Running in standalone mode
redis_1  |                                           Port: 6379
redis_1  |                                           PID: 1
redis_1  |
redis_1  |                                           http://redis.io
redis_1  |
redis_1  |
redis_1  |
redis_1  |
redis_1  |
redis_1  |
redis_1  |
redis_1  |   1:M 03 May 12:51:43.447 # WARNING: The TCP backlog setting of 511 cannot be enforced
because /proc/sys/net/core/somaxconn is set to the lower value of 128.
redis_1  |   1:M 03 May 12:51:43.447 # Server started, Redis version 3.2.8
redis_1  |   1:M 03 May 12:51:43.447 # WARNING overcommit_memory is set to 0! Background save may
fail under low memory condition. To fix this issue add 'vm.overcommit_memory = 1' to /etc/sysc
tl.conf and then reboot or run the command 'sysctl vm.overcommit_memory=1' for this to take eff
ect.
redis_1  |   1:M 03 May 12:51:43.447 # WARNING you have Transparent Huge Pages (THP) support enab
led in your kernel. This will create latency and memory usage issues with Redis. To fix this is
sue run the command 'echo never > /sys/kernel/mm/transparent_hugepage/enabled' as root, and add
it to your /etc/rc.local in order to retain the setting after a reboot. Redis must be restarte
d after THP is disabled.
redis_1  |   1:M 03 May 12:51:43.447 * The server is now ready to accept connections on port 6379
web_1    |  * Running on http://0.0.0.0:5000/ (Press CTRL+C to quit)
web_1    |  * Restarting with stat
web_1    |  * Debugger is active!
web_1    |  * Debugger PIN: 245-870-899
```

Now, we can see the output by following the running http url.

Output:

Hello World! I have been seen 1 times.

Each time, when we refresh the page. It shows counter incremented by 1.

Hello World! I have been seen 2 times.

Docker Storage Driver

Docker provides us pluggable storage driver architecture. It gives us the flexibility to "plug in" the storage driver in our Docker. It is completely bases on the Linux filesystem.

To implement, we must set driver at the docker daemon start time. The Docker daemon can only run one storage driver and all containers created by that daemon instance use the same storage driver.

The following table contains the Docker storage driver.

Technology	Storage driver name
OverlayFS	overlay or overlay2
AUFS	aufs
Btrfs	btrfs
Device Mapper	devicemapper
VFS	vfs
ZFS	zfs

Current Storage Driver

To check which storage driver is used by the daemon, we can use the following command.

```
$ docker info
```

```
root@irfan-GB-BXBT-2807: /home/irfan
root@irfan-GB-BXBT-2807:/home/irfan# docker info
Containers: 11
 Running: 0
 Paused: 0
 Stopped: 11
Images: 15
Server Version: 17.03.1-ce
Storage Driver: aufs
 Root Dir: /var/lib/docker/aufs
 Backing Filesystem: extfs
 Dirs: 53
 Dirperm1 Supported: true
Logging Driver: json-file
Cgroup Driver: cgroupfs
Plugins:
 Volume: local
 Network: bridge host macvlan null overlay
Swarm: inactive
Runtimes: runc
Default Runtime: runc
```

We can see that the above command shows the storage driver used by the daemon. The Backing Filesystem is extfs. The extfs means that the overlay storage driver is operating on the top of the filesystem.

The backing filesystem refers to the filesystem that was used to create the Docker host's local storage area under /var/lib/docker directory.

The following table contains storage drivers that must match the host?s backing filesystem.

Storage driver	Commonly used on	Disabled on
overlay	ext4xfs	btrfsaufsoverlayzfseCryptfs
overlay2	ext4xfs	btrfsaufsoverlayzfseCryptfs
aufs	ext4xfs	btrfsaufseCryptfs
btrfs	btrfsonly	N/A

devicemapper	Direct-lvm	N/A
vfs	debugging only	N/A
zfs	zfsonly	N/A

Note:- "Disabled on" means some storage drivers can not run over certain backing filesystem.

Setting Storage Driver

We can set storage driver by setting its name to the dockerd command. The following command starts a daemon and set new driver.

```
$ dockerd --storage-driver=devicemapper
```

Later on, we can check docker driver by the following command.

```
$ docker info
```

Docker Networking

Docker takes care of the networking aspects so that the containers can communicate with other containers and also with the Docker Host. If you do an ifconfig on the Docker Host, you will see the Docker Ethernet adapter. This adapter is created when Docker is installed on the Docker Host.

```
demo@ubuntudemo:~$ sudo ifconfig
docker0   Link encap:Ethernet  HWaddr 02:42:b4:a4:43:59
          inet addr:172.17.0.1  Bcast:0.0.0.0  Mask:255.255.0.0
          inet6 addr: fe80::42:b4ff:fea4:4359/64 Scope:Link
          UP BROADCAST MULTICAST  MTU:1500  Metric:1
          RX packets:55 errors:0 dropped:0 overruns:0 frame:0
          TX packets:28 errors:0 dropped:0 overruns:0 carrier:0
          collisions:0 txqueuelen:0
          RX bytes:3448 (3.4 KB)  TX bytes:2576 (2.5 KB)

eth0      Link encap:Ethernet  HWaddr 08:00:27:f5:15:76
          inet addr:192.168.137.200  Bcast:192.168.137.255  Mask:255.255.255.0
          inet6 addr: fe80::a00:27ff:fef5:1576/64 Scope:Link
          UP BROADCAST RUNNING MULTICAST  MTU:1500  Metric:1
          RX packets:199 errors:0 dropped:0 overruns:0 frame:0
          TX packets:70 errors:0 dropped:0 overruns:0 carrier:0
          collisions:0 txqueuelen:1000
          RX bytes:13734 (13.7 KB)  TX bytes:5238 (5.2 KB)

lo        Link encap:Local Loopback
          inet addr:127.0.0.1  Mask:255.0.0.0
          inet6 addr: ::1/128 Scope:Host
          UP LOOPBACK RUNNING  MTU:65536  Metric:1
          RX packets:40 errors:0 dropped:0 overruns:0 frame:0
          TX packets:40 errors:0 dropped:0 overruns:0 carrier:0
          collisions:0 txqueuelen:0
          RX bytes:3104 (3.1 KB)  TX bytes:3104 (3.1 KB)

demo@ubuntudemo:~$
```

This is a bridge between the Docker Host and the Linux Host. Now let's look at some commands associated with networking in Docker.

Listing All Docker Networks

This command can be used to list all the networks associated with Docker on the host.

The command will output all the networks on the Docker Host.

```
sudo docker network ls
```

Output

The output of the above command is shown below

```
demo@ubuntudemo:~$ sudo docker network ls
NETWORK ID          NAME                DRIVER              SCOPE
f07aad6ccadf        bridge              bridge              local
faae6bf679ea        host                host                local
54a2d37e7e00        none                null                local
demo@ubuntudemo:~$
```

Inspecting a Docker network

If you want to see more details on the network associated with Docker, you can use the Docker network inspect command.

Syntax

```
docker network inspect networkname
```

Options

networkname – This is the name of the network you need to inspect.

Return Value

The command will output all the details about the network.

Example

```
sudo docker network inspect bridge
```

Output

The output of the above command is shown below –

```
"Name": "bridge",
"Id": "f07aad6ccadf388082ccf9ad37db43f78adec85fb96ae0b2e9e8390c6d674242"

    "Scope": "local",
    "Driver": "bridge",
    "EnableIPv6": false,
    "IPAM": {
        "Driver": "default",
        "Options": null,
        "Config": [
            {
                "Subnet": "172.17.0.0/16",
                "Gateway": "172.17.0.1"
            }
        ]
    },
    "Internal": false,
    "Containers": {},
    "Options": {
        "com.docker.network.bridge.default_bridge": "true",
        "com.docker.network.bridge.enable_icc": "true",
        "com.docker.network.bridge.enable_ip_masquerade": "true",
        "com.docker.network.bridge.host_binding_ipv4": "0.0.0.0",
        "com.docker.network.bridge.name": "docker0",
        "com.docker.network.driver.mtu": "1500"
    },
    "Labels": {}
    }
]
demo@ubuntudemo:~$
```

Now let's run a container and see what happens when we inspect the network again. Let's spin up an Ubuntu container with the following command –

```
sudo docker run -it ubuntu:latest /bin/bash
```

```
demo@ubuntudemo:~$ sudo docker run -it ubuntu:latest /bin/bash
```

Now if we inspect our network name via the following command, you will now see that the container is attached to the bridge.

```
sudo docker network inspect bridge
```

```
                {
            "Subnet": "172.17.0.0/16",
            "Gateway": "172.17.0.1"
        }
    ]
},
"Internal": false,
"Containers": {
    "8e7b9a6dc121ba1c9a9fe48542db0149ee87b5efe031f518fb15751741ea0447":
    {
        "Name": "suspicious_blackwell",
        "EndpointID": "d30971d663e91ec2439355bb43c99613d500e35fbaae1957d
f74cb650f40723",
        "MacAddress": "02:42:ac:11:00:02",
        "IPv4Address": "172.17.0.2/16",
        "IPv6Address": ""
    }
},
"Options": {
    "com.docker.network.bridge.default_bridge": "true",
    "com.docker.network.bridge.enable_icc": "true",
    "com.docker.network.bridge.enable_ip_masquerade": "true",
    "com.docker.network.bridge.host_binding_ipv4": "0.0.0.0",
    "com.docker.network.bridge.name": "docker0",
    "com.docker.network.driver.mtu": "1500"
},
"Labels": {}
    }
]
emo@ubuntudemo:~$
```

Creating Your Own New Network

One can create a network in Docker before launching containers. This can be done with the following command —

Syntax

```
docker network create --driver drivername name
```

Options

- ❖ drivername — This is the name used for the network driver.
- ❖ name — This is the name given to the network.

Return Value

The command will output the long ID for the new network.

Example

```
sudo docker network create --driver bridge new_nw
```

Output

The output of the above command is shown below —

```
demo@ubuntudemo:~$ sudo docker network create --driver bridge new_nw
f01b64dc09425cc4906e20b5e17765e3248ea727068e0e2172bfc4aec42586fe
demo@ubuntudemo:~$ _
```

You can now attach the new network when launching the container. So let's spin up an Ubuntu container with the following command —

```
sudo docker run -it -network=new_nw ubuntu:latest
/bin/bash
```

```
demo@ubuntudemo:~$ sudo docker run -it --network=new_nw ubuntu:latest /bin/bash
```

And now when you inspect the network via the following command, you will see the container attached to the network.

```
sudo docker network inspect new_nw
```

```
"Scope": "local",
"Driver": "bridge",
"EnableIPv6": false,
"IPAM": {
    "Driver": "default",
    "Options": {},
    "Config": [
        {
            "Subnet": "172.18.0.0/16",
            "Gateway": "172.18.0.1/16"
        }
    ]
},
"Internal": false,
"Containers": {
    "38604fc42bcb5f78d42a8f40f34fa245301b2020a84c9e602786d2103ca6b847":
    {
        "Name": "boring_dubinsky",
        "EndpointID": "74d6b14a6393bf3081d5d9ec012b5b76b2ead49e85a5f664c
a621761a9e69612",
        "MacAddress": "02:42:ac:12:00:02",
        "IPv4Address": "172.18.0.2/16",
        "IPv6Address": ""
    }
},
"Options": {},
"Labels": {}
}
```

demo@ubuntudemo:~$

Setting Node .js

Node.js is a JavaScript framework that is used for developing server-side applications. It is an open source framework that is developed to run on a variety of operating systems. Since Node.js is a popular framework for development, Docker has also ensured it has support for Node.js applications.

We will now see the various steps for getting the Docker container for Node.js up and running.

Step 1 − The first step is to pull the image from Docker Hub. When you log into Docker Hub, you will be able to search and see the image for Node.js as shown below. Just type in Node in the search box and click on the node (official) link which comes up in the search results.

Step 2 − You will see that the Docker pull command for node in the details of the repository in Docker Hub.

Step 3 − On the Docker Host, use the Docker pull command as shown above to download the latest node image from Docker Hub.

```
demo@ubuntudemo:~$ sudo docker pull node_
```

Once the pull is complete, we can then proceed with the next step.

```
demo@ubuntudemo:~$ sudo docker pull node
Using default tag: latest
latest: Pulling from library/node

75a822cd7888: Downloading 31.54 MB/39.73 MB
75a822cd7888: Pull complete
57de64c72267: Pull complete
4306be1e8943: Pull complete
871436ab7225: Pull complete
9110c26a367a: Pull complete
1f04fe713f1b: Pull complete
723bac39028e: Pull complete
Digest: sha256:08d77f1984cf79739ba7c987636cb871fd69745754200e5891a0c7ee2d9965b0
Status: Downloaded newer image for node:latest
demo@ubuntudemo:~$
demo@ubuntudemo:~$
```

Step 4 – On the Docker Host, let's use the vim editor and create one Node.js example file. In this file, we will add a simple command to display "HelloWorld" to the command prompt.

```
demo@ubuntudemo:~$ vim HelloWorld.js
```

In the Node.js file, let's add the following statement –

```
Console.log('Hello World');
```

This will output the "Hello World" phrase when we run it through Node.js.

```
console.log('Hello World');_
```

Ensure that you save the file and then proceed to the next step.

Step 5 – To run our Node.js script using the Node Docker container, we need to execute the following statement –

```
sudo docker run −it −rm −name = HelloWorld −v
"$PWD":/usr/src/app
    −w /usr/src/app node node HelloWorld.js
```

The following points need to be noted about the above command −

- ❖ The −rm option is used to remove the container after it is run.
- ❖ We are giving a name to the container called "HelloWorld".
- ❖ We are mentioning to map the volume in the container which is /usr/src/app to our current present working directory. This is done so that the node container will pick up our HelloWorld.js script which is present in our working directory on the Docker Host.
- ❖ The −w option is used to specify the working directory used by Node.js.
- ❖ The first node option is used to specify to run the node image.
- ❖ The second node option is used to mention to run the node command in the node container.
- ❖ And finally we mention the name of our script.

We will then get the following output. And from the output, we can clearly see that the Node container ran as a container and executed the HelloWorld.js script.

```
demo@ubuntudemo:~$ sudo docker run -it --rm --name=HelloWorld -v "$PWD":/usr/s
/app -w /usr/src/app node node HelloWorld.js
Hello World
demo@ubuntudemo:~$
```

Setting MongoDB

MongoDB is a famous document-oriented database that is used by many modern-day web applications. Since MongoDB is a popular database for development, Docker has also ensured it has support for MongoDB.

We will now see the various steps for getting the Docker container for MongoDB up and running.

Step 1 − The first step is to pull the image from Docker Hub. When you log into Docker Hub, you will be able to search and see the image for Mongo as shown below. Just type in Mongo in the search box and click on the Mongo (official) link which comes up in the search results.

Step 2 − You will see that the Docker pull command for Mongo in the details of the repository in Docker Hub.

Step 3 − On the Docker Host, use the Docker pull command as shown above to download the latest Mongo image from Docker Hub.

```
demo@ubuntudemo:~$ sudo docker pull mongo
```

```
demo@ubuntudemo:~$ sudo docker pull mongo
[sudo] password for demo:
Using default tag: latest
latest: Pulling from library/mongo

75a822cd7888: Already exists
8bf369f658b6: Pull complete
7d7cb343d20e: Pull complete
73a933a908f7: Pull complete
658569c28c55: Pull complete
124a8bf940da: Pull complete
7c19551df503: Pull complete
a18347fe18d9: Pull complete
63e710c6ec29: Pull complete
Digest: sha256:23c5cdbd9bc26a6d1ae4db8252a295d6bdba8332dec60483816d5b7bb2438d7
Status: Downloaded newer image for mongo:latest
demo@ubuntudemo:~$
```

Step 4 – Now that we have the image for Mongo, let's first run a MongoDB container which will be our instance for MongoDB. For this, we will issue the following command –

```
sudo docker run -it -d mongo
```

The following points can be noted about the above command –

- ❖ The –it option is used to run the container in interactive mode.
- ❖ The –d option is used to run the container as a daemon process.
- ❖ And finally we are creating a container from the Mongo image.

You can then issue the docker ps command to see the running containers –

```
demo@ubuntudemo:~$ sudo docker run -it -d mongo
ec086eec7416e368614de631b8356fcf68eec978b01b620251cb55d8b7ec7189
demo@ubuntudemo:~$ sudo docker ps
CONTAINER ID      IMAGE       COMMAND                CREATED
    STATUS          PORTS            NAMES
ec086eec7416      mongo       "/entrypoint.sh mongo" 3 seconds ago
    Up 2 seconds    27017/tcp        tender_poitras
demo@ubuntudemo:~$ _
```

Take a note of the following points –

- ❖ The name of the container is tender_poitras. This name will be different since the name of the containers keep on changing when you spin up a container. But just make a note of the container which you have launched.
- ❖ Next, also notice the port number it is running on. It is listening on the TCP port of 27017.

Step 5 – Now let's spin up another container which will act as our client which will be used to connect to the MongoDB database. Let's issue the following command for this –

```
sudo docker run -it -link=tender_poitras:mongo mongo
/bin/bash
```

The following points can be noted about the above command –

❖ The –it option is used to run the container in interactive mode.

❖ We are now linking our new container to the already launched MongoDB server container. Here, you need to mention the name of the already launched container.

❖ We are then specifying that we want to launch the Mongo container as our client and then run the bin/bash shell in our new container.

```
demo@ubuntudemo:~$ sudo docker run -it --link=tender_poitras:mongo mongo /bin/
sh
root@83b6ae60e866:/#
```

You will now be in the new container.

Step 6 − Run the env command in the new container to see the details of how to connect to the MongoDB server container.

```
...
Server has startup warnings:
2017-01-07T15:26:23.769+0000 I STORAGE  [initandlisten]
2017-01-07T15:26:23.769+0000 I STORAGE  [initandlisten] ** WARNING: Using the
 filesystem is strongly recommended with the WiredTiger storage engine
2017-01-07T15:26:23.769+0000 I STORAGE  [initandlisten] **          See http:/
ochub.mongodb.org/core/prodnotes-filesystem
2017-01-07T15:26:23.873+0000 I CONTROL  [initandlisten]
2017-01-07T15:26:23.874+0000 I CONTROL  [initandlisten] ** WARNING: Access con
l is not enabled for the database.
2017-01-07T15:26:23.874+0000 I CONTROL  [initandlisten] **          Read and w
e access to data and configuration is unrestricted.
2017-01-07T15:26:23.874+0000 I CONTROL  [initandlisten]
2017-01-07T15:26:23.874+0000 I CONTROL  [initandlisten]
2017-01-07T15:26:23.875+0000 I CONTROL  [initandlisten] ** WARNING: /sys/kerne
mm/transparent_hugepage/enabled is 'always'.
2017-01-07T15:26:23.875+0000 I CONTROL  [initandlisten] **          We suggest s
ting it to 'never'
2017-01-07T15:26:23.875+0000 I CONTROL  [initandlisten]
2017-01-07T15:26:23.875+0000 I CONTROL  [initandlisten] ** WARNING: /sys/kerne
mm/transparent_hugepage/defrag is 'always'.
2017-01-07T15:26:23.875+0000 I CONTROL  [initandlisten] **          We suggest s
ting it to 'never'
2017-01-07T15:26:23.875+0000 I CONTROL  [initandlisten]
```

Step 6 − Now it's time to connect to the MongoDB server from the client container. We can do this via the following command −

```
mongo 172.17.0.2:27017
```

The following points need to be noted about the above command

pg. 107

❖ The mongo command is the client mongo command that is used to connect to a MongoDB database.

❖ The IP and port number is what you get when you use the env command.

Once you run the command, you will then be connected to the MongoDB database.

```
Server has startup warnings:
2017-01-07T15:26:23.769+0000 I STORAGE  [initandlisten]
2017-01-07T15:26:23.769+0000 I STORAGE  [initandlisten] ** WARNING: Using the
S filesystem is strongly recommended with the WiredTiger storage engine
2017-01-07T15:26:23.769+0000 I STORAGE  [initandlisten] **          See http:/
chub.mongodb.org/core/prodnotes-filesystem
2017-01-07T15:26:23.873+0000 I CONTROL  [initandlisten]
2017-01-07T15:26:23.874+0000 I CONTROL  [initandlisten] ** WARNING: Access con
1 is not enabled for the database.
2017-01-07T15:26:23.874+0000 I CONTROL  [initandlisten] **          Read and w
te access to data and configuration is unrestricted.
2017-01-07T15:26:23.874+0000 I CONTROL  [initandlisten]
2017-01-07T15:26:23.874+0000 I CONTROL  [initandlisten]
2017-01-07T15:26:23.875+0000 I CONTROL  [initandlisten] ** WARNING: /sys/kerne
mm/transparent_hugepage/enabled is 'always'.
2017-01-07T15:26:23.875+0000 I CONTROL  [initandlisten] **          We suggest s
ting it to 'never'
2017-01-07T15:26:23.875+0000 I CONTROL  [initandlisten]
2017-01-07T15:26:23.875+0000 I CONTROL  [initandlisten] ** WARNING: /sys/kerne
mm/transparent_hugepage/defrag is 'always'.
2017-01-07T15:26:23.875+0000 I CONTROL  [initandlisten] **          We suggest s
ting it to 'never'
2017-01-07T15:26:23.875+0000 I CONTROL  [initandlisten]
>
```

You can then run any MongoDB command in the command prompt. In our example, we are running the following command –

    use demo

This command is a MongoDB command which is used to switch to a database name demo. If the database is not available, it will be created.

```
2017-01-07T15:26:23.769+0000 I STORAGE  [initandlisten] ** WARNING: Using the
S filesystem is strongly recommended with the WiredTiger storage engine
2017-01-07T15:26:23.769+0000 I STORAGE  [initandlisten] **            See http:/
nchub.mongodb.org/core/prodnotes-filesystem
2017-01-07T15:26:23.873+0000 I CONTROL  [initandlisten]
2017-01-07T15:26:23.874+0000 I CONTROL  [initandlisten] ** WARNING: Access con
ol is not enabled for the database.
2017-01-07T15:26:23.874+0000 I CONTROL  [initandlisten] **            Read and w
te access to data and configuration is unrestricted.
2017-01-07T15:26:23.874+0000 I CONTROL  [initandlisten]
2017-01-07T15:26:23.874+0000 I CONTROL  [initandlisten]
2017-01-07T15:26:23.875+0000 I CONTROL  [initandlisten] ** WARNING: /sys/kerne
mm/transparent_hugepage/enabled is 'always'.
2017-01-07T15:26:23.875+0000 I CONTROL  [initandlisten] **            We suggest s
ting it to 'never'
2017-01-07T15:26:23.875+0000 I CONTROL  [initandlisten]
2017-01-07T15:26:23.875+0000 I CONTROL  [initandlisten] ** WARNING: /sys/kerne
mm/transparent_hugepage/defrag is 'always'.
2017-01-07T15:26:23.875+0000 I CONTROL  [initandlisten] **            We suggest s
ting it to 'never'
2017-01-07T15:26:23.875+0000 I CONTROL  [initandlisten]
> use demo
switched to db demo
>
```

Now you have successfully created a client and server MongoDB container.

Setting NGINX

NGINX is a popular lightweight web application that is used for developing server-side applications. It is an open-source web server that is developed to run on a variety of operating systems. Since nginx is a popular web server for development, Docker has ensured that it has support for nginx.

We will now see the various steps for getting the Docker container for nginx up and running.

Step 1 – The first step is to pull the image from Docker Hub. When you log into Docker Hub, you will be able to search and see the image for nginx as shown below. Just type in nginx in the search box and click on the nginx (official) link which comes up in the search results.

Step 2 – You will see that the Docker pull command for nginx in the details of the repository in Docker Hub.

Step 3 – On the Docker Host, use the Docker pull command as shown above to download the latest nginx image from Docker Hub.

```
demo@ubuntudemo:~$ sudo docker pull nginx
Using default tag: latest
latest: Pulling from library/nginx

75a822cd7888: Already exists
0aefb9dc4a57: Pull complete
046e44ee6057: Pull complete
Digest: sha256:fab482910aae9630c93bd24fc6fcecb9f9f792c24a8974f5e46d8ad625ac235
Status: Downloaded newer image for nginx:latest
demo@ubuntudemo:~$ _
```

Step 4 – Now let's run the nginx container via the following command.

```
sudo docker run –p 8080:80 –d nginx
```

We are exposing the port on the nginx server which is port 80 to the port 8080 on the Docker Host.

Once you run the command, you will get the following output if you browse to the URL http://dockerhost:8080. This shows that the nginx container is up and running.

Step 5 − Let's look at another example where we can host a simple web page in our ngnix container. In our example, we will create a simple HelloWorld.html file and host it in our nginx container.

Let's first create an HTML file called HelloWorld.html

Let's add a simple line of Hello World in the HTML file.

Let's then run the following Docker command.

```
sudo docker run -p 8080:80 -v
   "$PWD":/usr/share/nginx/html:ro -d nginx
```

The following points need to be noted about the above command –

❖ We are exposing the port on the nginx server which is port 80 to the port 8080 on the Docker Host.

❖ Next, we are attaching the volume on the container which is /usr/share/nginx/html to our present working directory. This is where our HelloWorld.html file is stored.

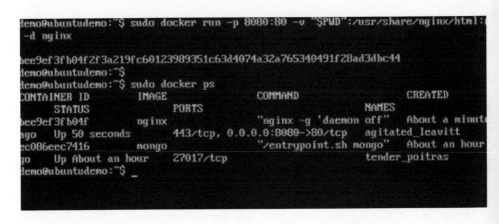

Now if we browse to the
URL http://dockerhost:8080/HelloWorld.html we will get the following output as expected –

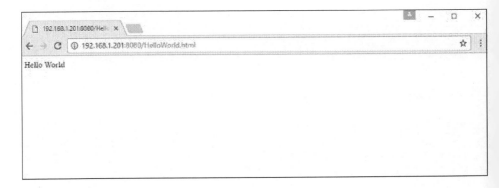

Setting ASP.Net

ASP.Net is the standard web development framework that is provided by Microsoft for developing server-side applications. Since ASP.Net has been around for quite a long time for development, Docker has ensured that it has support for ASP.Net.

In this chapter, we will see the various steps for getting the Docker container for ASP.Net up and running.

Prerequisites

The following steps need to be carried out first for running ASP.Net.

Step 1 − Since this can only run on Windows systems, you first need to ensure that you have either Windows 10 or Window Server 2016.

Step 2 − Next, ensure that Hyper-V is and Containers are installed on the Windows system. To install Hyper–V and Containers, you can go to Turn Windows Features ON or OFF. Then ensure the Hyper-V option and Containers is checked and click the OK button.

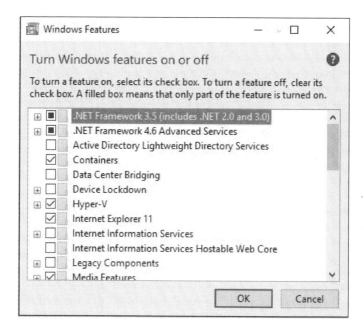

The system might require a restart after this operation.

Step 3 – Next, you need to use the following Powershell command to install the 1.13.0rc4 version of Docker. The following command will download this and store it in the temp location.

```
Invoke-WebRequest
"https://test.docker.com/builds/Windows/x86_64/docker-
1.13.0-
    rc4.zip" -OutFile "$env:TEMP\docker-1.13.0-rc4.zip" –
UseBasicParsing
```

Step 4 – Next, you need to expand the archive using the following powershell command.

```
Expand-Archive -Path "$env:TEMP\docker-1.13.0-rc4.zip" -
DestinationPath $env:ProgramFiles
```

Step 5 – Next, you need to add the Docker Files to the environment variable using the following powershell command.

```
$env:path += ";$env:ProgramFiles\Docker"
```

Step 6 – Next, you need to register the Docker Daemon Service using the following powershell command.

```
dockerd --register-service
```

Step 7 – Finally, you can start the docker daemon using the following command.

```
Start-Service Docker
```

Use the docker version command in powershell to verify that the docker daemon is working

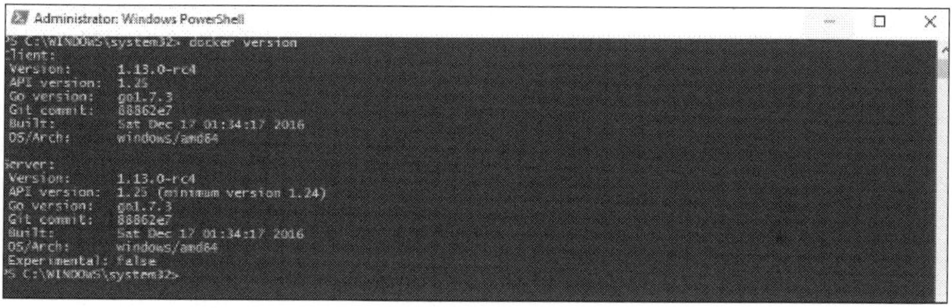

Installing the ASP.Net Container

Let's see how to install the ASP.Net container.

Step 1 – The first step is to pull the image from Docker Hub. When you log into Docker Hub, you will be able to search and see the image for Microsoft/aspnet as shown below. Just type in asp in the search box and click on the Microsoft/aspnet link which comes up in the search results.

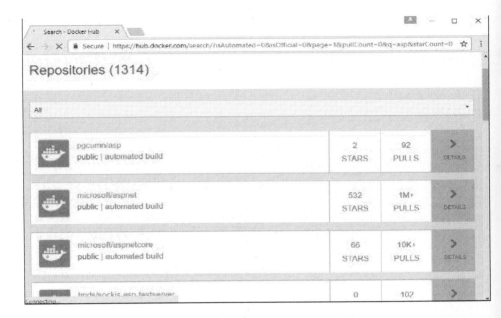

Step 2 – You will see that the Docker pull command for ASP.Net in the details of the repository in Docker Hub.

Step 3 – Go to Docker Host and run the Docker pull command for the microsoft/aspnet image. Note that the image is pretty large, somewhere close to 4.2 GB.

Step 4 – Now go to the following location https://github.com/Microsoft/aspnet-docker and download the entire Git repository.

Step 5 – Create a folder called App in your C drive. Then copy the contents from the 4.6.2/sample folder to your C drive. Go the Docker File in the sample directory and issue the following command –

```
docker build -t aspnet-site-new –build-arg site_root=/
```

The following points need to be noted about the above command –

- It builds a new image called aspnet-site-new from the Docker File.
- The root path is set to the localpath folder.

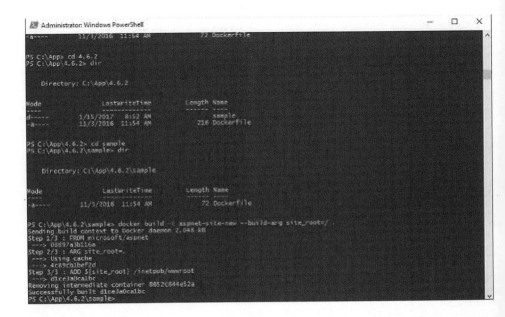

Step 6 – Now it's time to run the container. It can be done using the following command –

```
docker run –d –p 8000:80 –name my-running-site-new aspnet-
site-new
```

Step 7 – You will now have IIS running in the Docker container. To find the IP Address of the Docker container, you can issue the Docker inspect command as shown below.

Docker Logging

Docker has logging mechanisms in place which can be used to debug issues as and when they occur. There is logging at the daemon level and at the container level. Let's look at the different levels of logging.

Daemon Logging

At the daemon logging level, there are four levels of logging available —

   ❖ Debug — It details all the possible information handled by the daemon process.
   ❖ Info — It details all the errors + Information handled by the daemon process.
   ❖ Errors — It details all the errors handled by the daemon process.
   ❖ Fatal — It only details all the fatal errors handled by the daemon process.

Go through the following steps to learn how to enable logging.

Step 1 — First, we need to stop the docker daemon process, if it is already running. It can be done using the following command —

```
sudo service docker stop
```

```
demo@ubuntudemo:~$ sudo service docker stop
```

Step 2 — Now we need to start the docker daemon process. But this time, we need to append the –l parameter to specify the logging option. So let's issue the following command when starting the docker daemon process.

```
sudo dockerd –l debug &
```

The following points need to be noted about the above command —

- ❖ dockerd is the executable for the docker daemon process.
- ❖ The –l option is used to specify the logging level. In our case, we are putting this as debug
- ❖ & is used to come back to the command prompt after the logging has been enabled.

```
demo@ubuntudemo:~$ sudo dockerd -l debug &
```

Once you start the Docker process with logging, you will also now see the Debug Logs being sent to the console.

```
DEBU[0001] Registering POST, /build
DEBU[0001] Registering POST, /swarm/init
DEBU[0001] Registering POST, /swarm/join
DEBU[0001] Registering POST, /swarm/leave
DEBU[0001] Registering GET, /swarm
DEBU[0001] Registering POST, /swarm/update
DEBU[0001] Registering GET, /services
DEBU[0001] Registering GET, /services/{id:.*}
DEBU[0001] Registering POST, /services/create
DEBU[0001] Registering POST, /services/{id:.*}/update
DEBU[0001] Registering DELETE, /services/{id:.*}
DEBU[0001] Registering GET, /nodes
DEBU[0001] Registering GET, /nodes/{id:.*}
DEBU[0001] Registering DELETE, /nodes/{id:.*}
DEBU[0001] Registering POST, /nodes/{id:.*}/update
DEBU[0001] Registering GET, /tasks
DEBU[0001] Registering GET, /tasks/{id:.*}
DEBU[0001] Registering GET, /networks
DEBU[0001] Registering GET, /networks/{id:.*}
DEBU[0001] Registering POST, /networks/create
DEBU[0001] Registering POST, /networks/{id:.*}/connect
DEBU[0001] Registering POST, /networks/{id:.*}/disconnect
DEBU[0001] Registering DELETE, /networks/{id:.*}
INFO[0001] API listen on /var/run/docker.sock
DEBU[0003] libcontainerd: containerd connection state change: READY
```

Now, if you execute any Docker command such as docker images, the Debug information will also be sent to the console.

```
demo@ubuntudemo:~$ sudo docker images
DEBU[0089] Calling GET /v1.24/images/json
REPOSITORY              TAG              IMAGE ID          CREATED
SIZE
node                    latest           7c4d899628d5      3 days ago
660.4 MB
nginx                   latest           01f818af747d      11 days ago
181.6 MB
mongo                   latest           a3bfb96cf65e      2 weeks ago
402 MB
web                     latest           f5792fc30aaa      2 weeks ago
267.9 MB
firstweb                latest           0e52e236368a      2 weeks ago
267.6 MB
ubuntu                  latest           104bec311bcd      3 weeks ago
129 MB
jenkins                 latest           ff6f0051ef57      5 weeks ago
714.1 MB
demo@ubuntudemo:~$ _
```

Container Logging

Logging is also available at the container level. So in our example, let's spin up an Ubuntu container first. We can do it by using the following command.

```
sudo docker run -it ubuntu /bin/bash
```

```
demo@ubuntudemo:~$ sudo docker run -it ubuntu /bin/bash
root@6bfb1271fcdd:/# demo@ubuntudemo:~$
demo@ubuntudemo:~$
```

Now, we can use the docker log command to see the logs of the container.

Syntax

```
Docker logs containerID
```

Parameters

❖ containerID – This is the ID of the container for which you need to see the logs.

Example

On our Docker Host, let's issue the following command. Before that, you can issue some commands whilst in the container.

| sudo docker logs 6bfb1271fcdd

Output

```
demo@ubuntudemo:~$ sudo docker logs 6bfb1271fcdd
root@6bfb1271fcdd:/#
root@6bfb1271fcdd:/# ifconfig
bash: ifconfig: command not found
root@6bfb1271fcdd:/# ls
bin    dev   home  lib64  mnt  proc  run    srv  tmp  var
boot   etc   lib   media  opt  root  sbin   sys  usr
demo@ubuntudemo:~$
```

From the output, you can see that the commands executed in the container are shown in the logs.

Kubernetes Architecture

Kubernetes is an orchestration framework for Docker containers which helps expose containers as services to the outside world. For example, you can have two services — One service would contain nginx and mongoDB, and another service would contain nginx and redis. Each service can have an IP or service point which can be connected by other applications. Kubernetes is then used to manage these services.

The following diagram shows in a simplistic format how Kubernetes works from an architecture point of view.

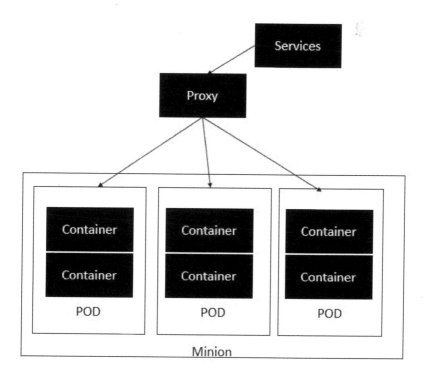

The minion is the node on which all the services run. You can have many minions running at one point in time. Each minion will host one or more POD. Each POD is like hosting a service. Each POD then contains the Docker containers. Each POD can host a different set of

Docker containers. The proxy is then used to control the exposing of these services to the outside world.

Kubernetes has several components in its architecture. The role of each component is explained below &mius;

❖ etcd – This component is a highly available key-value store that is used for storing shared configuration and service discovery. Here the various applications will be able to connect to the services via the discovery service.

❖ Flannel – This is a backend network which is required for the containers.

❖ kube-apiserver – This is an API which can be used to orchestrate the Docker containers.

❖ kube-controller-manager – This is used to control the Kubernetes services.

❖ kube-scheduler – This is used to schedule the containers on hosts.

❖ Kubelet – This is used to control the launching of containers via manifest files.

❖ kube-proxy – This is used to provide network proxy services to the outside world.

Working on Kubernetes

In this chapter, we will see how to install Kubenetes via kubeadm. This is a tool which helps in the installation of Kubernetes. Let's go step by step and learn how to install Kubernetes.

Step 1 − Ensure that the Ubuntu server version you are working on is 16.04.

Step 2 − Ensure that you generate a ssh key which can be used for ssh login. You can do this using the following command.

```
ssh-keygen
```

This will generate a key in your home folder as shown below.

```
master@master:~$ ssh-keygen
Generating public/private rsa key pair.
Enter file in which to save the key (/home/master/.ssh/id_rsa):
Created directory '/home/master/.ssh'.
Enter passphrase (empty for no passphrase):
Enter same passphrase again:
Your identification has been saved in /home/master/.ssh/id_rsa.
Your public key has been saved in /home/master/.ssh/id_rsa.pub.
The key fingerprint is:
SHA256:a30Av0xfNvituylJsTZRt71keq90hrp7qUSjqSo5w04 master@master
The key's randomart image is:
+----[RSA 2048]----+
|                  |
|                  |
|      . .         |
|     . .. o .     |
|    o S+oo o      |
|    . .oBo...+    |
|  .  o.Bo*o.=o.   |
|  .*  . ooB+++oo  |
|  .E+..o...BB.ooo.|
+----[SHA256]-----+
master@master:~$ _
```

Step 3 − Next, depending on the version of Ubuntu you have, you will need to add the relevant site to the docker.list for the apt package manager, so that it will be able to detect the Kubernetes packages from the kubernetes site and download them accordingly.

We can do it using the following commands.

```
curl -s https://packages.cloud.google.com/apt/doc/apt-
key.gpg | apt-key add -
echo "deb http://apt.kubernetes.io/ kubernetes-xenial
main" | sudo tee /etc/apt/sources.list.d/docker.list
```

Step 4 – We then issue an apt-get update to ensure all packages are downloaded on the Ubuntu server.

```
Get:25 http://us.archive.ubuntu.com/ubuntu xenial/universe amd64 Packages [7,532 kB]
Get:26 http://us.archive.ubuntu.com/ubuntu xenial/universe i386 Packages [7,512 kB]
Get:27 http://us.archive.ubuntu.com/ubuntu xenial/universe Translation-en [4,354 kB]
Get:28 http://us.archive.ubuntu.com/ubuntu xenial/multiverse amd64 Packages [144 kB]
Get:29 http://us.archive.ubuntu.com/ubuntu xenial/multiverse i386 Packages [140 kB]
Get:30 http://us.archive.ubuntu.com/ubuntu xenial/multiverse Translation-en [106 kB]
Get:31 http://us.archive.ubuntu.com/ubuntu xenial-updates/main amd64 Packages [452 kB]
Get:32 http://us.archive.ubuntu.com/ubuntu xenial-updates/main i386 Packages [444 kB]
Get:33 http://us.archive.ubuntu.com/ubuntu xenial-updates/main Translation-en [178 kB]
Get:34 http://us.archive.ubuntu.com/ubuntu xenial-updates/restricted amd64 Packages [6,576 B]
Get:35 http://us.archive.ubuntu.com/ubuntu xenial-updates/restricted i386 Packages [6,520 B]
Get:36 http://us.archive.ubuntu.com/ubuntu xenial-updates/restricted Translation-en [2,016 B]
Get:37 http://us.archive.ubuntu.com/ubuntu xenial-updates/universe amd64 Packages [378 kB]
Get:38 http://us.archive.ubuntu.com/ubuntu xenial-updates/universe i386 Packages [373 kB]
Get:39 http://us.archive.ubuntu.com/ubuntu xenial-updates/universe Translation-en [140 kB]
Get:40 http://us.archive.ubuntu.com/ubuntu xenial-updates/multiverse amd64 Packages [7,384 B]
Get:41 http://us.archive.ubuntu.com/ubuntu xenial-updates/multiverse i386 Packages [6,180 B]
Get:42 http://us.archive.ubuntu.com/ubuntu xenial-updates/multiverse Translation-en [3,080 B]
Get:43 http://us.archive.ubuntu.com/ubuntu xenial-backports/main amd64 Packages [4,404 B]
Get:44 http://us.archive.ubuntu.com/ubuntu xenial-backports/main i386 Packages [4,404 B]
Get:45 http://us.archive.ubuntu.com/ubuntu xenial-backports/main Translation-en [3,124 B]
Get:46 http://us.archive.ubuntu.com/ubuntu xenial-backports/universe amd64 Packages [2,412 B]
Get:47 http://us.archive.ubuntu.com/ubuntu xenial-backports/universe i386 Packages [2,412 B]
Get:48 http://us.archive.ubuntu.com/ubuntu xenial-backports/universe Translation-en [1,216 B]
Fetched 26.0 MB in 57s (455 kB/s)
Reading package lists... Done
root@slave:~#
```

Step 5 – Install the Docker package as detailed in the earlier chapters.

Step 6 – Now it's time to install kubernetes by installing the following packages –

```
apt-get install –y kubelet kubeadm kubectl kubernetes-cni
```

```
root@slave:~# apt-get install -y kubelet kubeadm kubectl kubernetes-cni_
```

```
Preparing to unpack .../kubernetes-cni_0.3.0.1-07a8a2-00_amd64.deb ...
Unpacking kubernetes-cni (0.3.0.1-07a8a2-00) ...
Selecting previously unselected package socat.
Preparing to unpack .../socat_1.7.3.1-1_amd64.deb ...
Unpacking socat (1.7.3.1-1) ...
Selecting previously unselected package kubelet.
Preparing to unpack .../kubelet_1.5.1-00_amd64.deb ...
Unpacking kubelet (1.5.1-00) ...
Selecting previously unselected package kubectl.
Preparing to unpack .../kubectl_1.5.1-00_amd64.deb ...
Unpacking kubectl (1.5.1-00) ...
Selecting previously unselected package kubeadm.
Preparing to unpack .../kubeadm_1.6.0-alpha.0-2074-a092d8e0f95f52-00_amd64.deb ...
Unpacking kubeadm (1.6.0-alpha.0-2074-a092d8e0f95f52-00) ...
Processing triggers for systemd (229-4ubuntu7) ...
Processing triggers for ureadahead (0.100.0-19) ...
Processing triggers for man-db (2.7.5-1) ...
Setting up ebtables (2.0.10.4-3.4ubuntu1) ...
update-rc.d: warning: start and stop actions are no longer supported: falling back to defaults
Setting up kubernetes-cni (0.3.0.1-07a8a2-00) ...
Setting up socat (1.7.3.1-1) ...
Setting up kubelet (1.5.1-00) ...
Setting up kubectl (1.5.1-00) ...
Setting up kubeadm (1.6.0-alpha.0-2074-a092d8e0f95f52-00) ...
Processing triggers for systemd (229-4ubuntu7) ...
Processing triggers for ureadahead (0.100.0-19) ...
root@slave:~#
```

Step 7 – Once all kubernetes packages are downloaded, it's time to start the kubernetes controller using the following command –

```
kubeadm init
```

```
[kubeconfig] Wrote KubeConfig file to disk: /etc/kubernetes/admin.conf
[apiclient] Created API client, waiting for the control plane to become ready
[apiclient] All control plane components are healthy after 113.293014 seconds
[apiclient] Waiting for at least one node to register and become ready
[apiclient] First node is ready after 6.502838 seconds
[apiclient] Creating a test deployment
[apiclient] Test deployment succeeded
[token-discovery] Created the kube-discovery deployment, waiting for it to become ready
[token-discovery] kube-discovery is ready after 55.503574 seconds
[addons] Created essential addon: kube-proxy
[addons] Created essential addon: kube-dns

Your Kubernetes master has initialized successfully!

You should now deploy a pod network to the cluster.
Run "kubectl apply -f [podnetwork].yaml" with one of the options listed at:
    http://kubernetes.io/docs/admin/addons/

You can now join any number of machines by running the following on each node:

kubeadm join --token=101573.c17ba345fc84fb71 192.168.1.105
root@slave:~# _
```

Once done, you will get a successful message that the master is up and running and nodes can now join the cluster.

Printed in Great Britain
by Amazon